CATHERINE EDM   ort
story writer and nc   er up
in the Circaidy Gi   raphy
Challenge.

By the same author

wormwood, earth and honey
Small Poisons
Serpentine
Bacchus Wynd

CATHERINE EDMUNDS

MY HIDDEN MOTHER

Catherine Edmunds

To my mother.

CONTENTS

PART ONE

PART TWO

PART THREE

Appendix I

Appendix II

Appendix III

I find that people in this country haven't a clue really what happened, in spite of all that has been said. They still haven't a clue what was going on. And it seems strange to me. And for instance, a woman in the rambling club, when I said I wouldn't be out today, because of being interviewed about my wartime experiences, said: "What wartime experiences? You were a child!" That to me is very odd. I didn't bother to explain. But after all, even an English child had wartime experiences, whether they were evacuated, or whatever, but this absolute lack of knowledge of what went on...

Jana Tanner, née Gráfová

This is the story of *what went on.*

8

PART ONE

1

SAILING OUT OF THE PARK

Three small children, Jana, Pavel and Jirka, cross the border from their home in Bratislava to visit Aunt Herma in Vienna. They are taken for a treat to the famous *Prater* funfair, where they paddle a small boat around a make-believe Viennese Venice. The adults have decided the newly-opened ghost train will be too frightening for the little ones, but the boat should be fine. The adults can't foresee what is about to happen. The children reach a blocked gate and are stuck. The youngest, Jana, is terrified.

Their teenage half-sister Máňa isn't with them to sort them out and offer advice or rescue. She has accompanied the family on this trip to Vienna in the hope that Aunt Herma's sons, Gusti and Dolfi, will take her shopping. Boys being boys, they have no interest in shopping and have taken her instead to a political meeting. This is Austria in the mid nineteen-thirties, so naturally, given the situation in neighbouring Germany, there are a lot of political meetings.

Back in the *Prater*, the eldest brother, Jirka, takes control in his big sister's absence. He shouts at the gate and bangs it with the boat, then with a paddle. He is strong-willed, and insists on being let through. Jirka tends to get his way, so the gate opens at last and they manage to continue. Jana is relieved, but perhaps this is a bad time to be sailing forth so decisively.

And here the memory stops, because this is not my memory; it belongs to my mother, Jana, and she's trying to think back nearly eighty years to dredge up the past. I want to help, but I know I'll muddle things up with the benefit of hindsight; the knowledge – which is still somewhat sketchy at this point – of what is going to happen to the children, to their parents, to Herma and her sons, over the next few years. I've been to Vienna, but the Vienna I knew in the nineteen-seventies will be very different to the city my mother visited in the thirties. I suspect our only common ground is a mutual fondness for Wiener Schnitzel and a memory of grand buildings and trams. There's another problem. I've received an email from my Uncle Paul – Jana's brother Pavel, the middle one of the three children – and his memories of this trip to Vienna are very different to my mother's. He has no recollection of a boat on a lake, but has told me about the ghost train, so it turns out they went on the ride after all. According to Paul, the children sat in a small rail car that went along a mostly indoor track, up and down, and even through water, with frightening figures looming up all around them. I love fairground ghost trains, and can picture this perfectly.

So which memory is the true one? Both? Neither? I can imagine Jana not being allowed on the ghost train as she was a little girl and the adults would have assumed it was too scary for her; but I can equally imagine the two older boys begging to go on it and jumping up and down with glee when told they could. Paul's memory of the train may have displaced that of the gentler boat ride which made such an impression on Jana, but perhaps her fear is picking up on the terror her brothers may have described when talking about the ghost train. I don't know how to begin disentangling the memories at this distance, but I'm going to have to make the effort if I'm to find out who my mother really is and what happened in her childhood to make her the person she is now.

I try another tack. Mother and I are chatting on the phone when I mention the dog; a German Shepherd.

'German Shepherd?' she says. 'It was a chihuahua!'

No, not that one. I know about the chihuahua. I'm talking about the German Shepherd that lived in the apartment block in Bratislava, the dog her two brothers and their friends played with, the one that took their orders – sit! Stay! That sort of thing. No, she says, there wasn't a German Shepherd. She thinks I'm confusing it with her half-sister Máňa's chihuahua, given to her by a boyfriend but not made welcome at home because their father, Gustav, wasn't a dog person. Why do I think there was a German Shepherd? Because her brother Paul has told me about in reply to an email of mine where I was asking him about his early life. He was very clear about this particular dog.

As Paul is nearly two and a half years older than Jana, she concedes that his memories of the very early days may be clearer than hers; there may have been this animal, but she has her doubts. I don't get any further with the dog. I wonder why Gustav, the children's father, didn't like dogs. I'm not keen myself. Maybe I've inherited his dislike of all things canine. I know he liked collecting stamps and paintings and Dresden figurines. I've collected stamps and I'm an artist, so I hold onto this, trying to find connections with the grandfather I never knew and who I can only picture from the few old photos that have survived showing a small dapper man with a neat goatee beard. I've drawn a portrait of him which I've given to my mother as a gift, and she says she is astonished by the likeness. This gives me hope that I'm managing to immerse myself in my mother's past, that I really am going to be able to find out about her early life. I'm going to have to pick up clues as best I can, and where different memories collide perhaps I'll be able to use the sort of genetic sixth sense that enabled me to draw an accurate portrait from a few tiny photos.

I need to go back to the beginning, to sort out the facts as far as I can. I thought I already knew my mother's background, but it's becoming clear that that's not the case. When my brother and I were very young, Mother would sometimes talk to us about her childhood experiences but much of it seemed so nightmarish I was nervous of asking questions and the conversations were never taken very far. I enjoyed the story of the teacher and the grass snake, and the wicked nuns, but didn't like to ask about the genuinely scary stuff. My cousin Charles, Máňa's son, knows even less than I do. When I phoned him to pick his brains about our shared background, he told me he never talked to his parents about what had happened to them when he was in his teens because teenagers don't – I know what he means – and then when he was much older, and wanted to know, it was too late.

This non-asking is typical of children in our position. A Jewish friend of mine has said I'm a classic second generation holocaust survivor, wanting to protect my mother by not asking too much; not dragging up memories I assume she would sooner keep hidden, but I'm not convinced. Some say that if I start asking questions now, it could prove emotionally draining for all concerned and that therefore it might not be a wise thing to do. That might well be the case if Mother had never talked about her life before, but she has – not especially to me and my brother, but certainly to anyone wanting to research the holocaust, as well as to her U3A class on aural history. She's even provided material for the historian Sir Martin Gilbert, who mentions her in his book *The Righteous: The Unsung Heroes of the Holocaust*. I wonder if all these people – historians I've never met, university students, various researchers, her friends at the U3A – know more about my family history than I do, but no, they can't know the minutiae of family experience that I must have been told when young; memories that need to be dredged up from my own subconscious as much as my mother's.

It's clear that I'm going to have to turn detective to find out as much as I can while there are still memories to be found. I'm going to pick my mother's brains, and when her memories dry up, I'm going to kick start them with anything I can find out from her brother Paul, from the memoirs of her childhood friend Gerda, her cousin Marian, or anyone else I can discover with a connection to her story. It will be slow going. Mother sends me notes in a spidery longhand that I can't always read. 'Am I writing this whole book for you?' she asks, having sent a couple of thousand words of notes and thinking this comprises an entire book. No, Mother. You're not. 'Will people outside the immediate family even be interested?' Yes they will. Come on Mum. Don't get cold feet.

Uncle Paul sends emails from New Jersey which are easier to read, but his health is poor and it is sometimes difficult for him to continue the correspondence. My mother can't email. She's internet-wary, despite being no technophobe in other respects. She could always programme the latest video-recorder with ease, so I don't know why she's never embraced the internet age, but that's how it is, and there's nothing I can do about it.

Back to the narrative. Three small children sail out of a gate in Vienna's *Prater*, out of the thirties, out of a fairy-tale childhood full of parks and kite-flying, puppet theatres, books and music – and into chaos. To say their world will be changed forever is facile. Of course it will, but more importantly, the children will be changed. Their paths will diverge dramatically. I can't follow them all because not all can be followed, so I'm going to concentrate on just one; Jana. I'm going to search for my hidden mother. I'll need to find background information that has been destroyed, tease out memories that have been suppressed – and I have no idea how the process is going to affect either my mother or myself.

2

GUSTAV

Some background first. Inspired by drawing the portrait, I'll start with my grandfather, Gustav Graf. The photos I have are in black and white, but I'm told he had a ginger moustache and white beard. I know he was an engineer, he liked art, didn't like dogs. That's all I know. This is where the research begins.

From my mother's notes I have learnt that Gustav was born in 1881 in Malšovice, a suburb of Hradec Králové in what is now the Czech Republic. The family comprised father Leopold, who worked in the estate office; mother Anna; older sister Hermina/Wilhelmina (who Jana would later know as Aunt Herma in Vienna); older brother Emil, and younger sister Berta. My mother hasn't been able to give me much information about Gustav's childhood, though she knows he was educated at the local technical college where he attained a degree in engineering. This qualified him to precede his name with the title 'Ing.' He'd originally wanted to be an artist, but had come under parental pressure to qualify in something more likely to earn him a living. I know the feeling. I was strongly drawn to art as a small child and cannot remember a time when I didn't have a chubby wax crayon in my hand – but when it came to making choices in my late teens, I was encouraged to go into music rather than art, so that's what I did. Gustav and I both had pragmatic parents, it would seem.

I managed to keep my art going as a hobby, but Gustav's artistic leanings led him to collect paintings by contemporary Slovak artists, as well as Dresden figurines, Czech glass ornaments, and anything else that caught his eye. This did not always go down well at home. His wife, Kamila, often complained that there wasn't enough space in the flat for all these bits and pieces, and the money could have been better spent on more practical things, but he was never deterred. He also provided a critique, whether wanted or not, of his children's early attempts at drawing. I like to think the criticism was helpful rather than harsh, my evidence being a pencil drawing his eldest daughter Máňa would make years later of my mother in which the likeness is unmistakeable.

Czechoslovakia wasn't covered by the O level geography syllabus when I was at school, so that's my excuse for never having heard of either Malšovice or Hradec Králové. My out-of-date atlas doesn't help. When I started writing this biography I soon realised that I would have to develop a strategy for familiarising myself with places I could barely pronounce let alone picture in my mind's eye. The solution was in front of me as I typed. The internet may be the 'web of lies' but it also has useful resources. I started with Google maps, to give myself a rough idea of where everywhere was in relation to everywhere else, and then headed over to YouTube to hunt down old film clips of relevant parts of the old Austro-Hungarian Empire. I discovered Vienna was well-documented, as was Prague, with a wealth of helpful home movies and professionally produced travelogues for both cities. It soon became apparent that it would be harder to find visual references for the smaller towns and villages, especially pre-1930. When I looked for Hradec Králové, I failed at first to find any contemporary photographic evidence other than a 1915 postcard of an impressive-looking Baroque synagogue. I took this as my lead, and tried to find out more about the building. Either it would have been destroyed by now, or if it had survived, would have found some other use. I was right. Further research revealed that by the end of the sixties, this synagogue had fallen into a state of complete disrepair, but luckily it was renovated in the early seventies and turned into a reference library. I think Gustav would have approved of this new use. I took a stroll around the area using Google's very handy 'street view' to get a contemporary view of the building. The Hebrew writing high up on one side is still intact, and in modern Hebrew intonation would sound like this: *be'beit elohim ne-ha'leich be'regesh*. These words are taken from Psalm 55, and can be translated as: 'We walked in the house of God in a crowd filled with emotion'. The trees on either side of the inscription are either *eshel avraham*, Abraham's trees, signifying hospitality, or they could represent the Tree of Life – the Torah. Two sticks either side could be Moses' and Aaron's staffs, and the metal *magen-david* (star of David) on the top of the building no doubt acts as a lightning conductor. Comparing the modern view with the vintage postcard, it's clear that the exterior has been faithfully restored; the only difference being the signs to the restaurants in the basement. Gustav must have seen this building in his youth, though whether he ever went inside I have no idea. Although he came from a Jewish background, he had rejected the faith and was a lifelong atheist. I've asked my mother, but she has no idea if his parents were practising Jews or not. The more I found out about my grandfather, the more it became clear that this atheism was a defining feature of his character. In later days, when others might turn to their faith for solace, he remained convinced of the rationality and importance of his own stance.

Having achieved a sense of 'place', I next tried to get more of a sense of the people that lived here. The internet helpfully provided a list of famous names from the area, some of them very well known. Gustav was born in Hradec Králové just six years before the Josef Čapek, the artist and writer who first coined the word 'robot', which would later be used by his brother Karel, and then, famously, by Isaac Asimov – who was born in 1920, the same year the word first appeared. I'm a keen science fiction fan, but my mother can't abide either sci-fi or fantasy, two genres that she dislikes on the grounds that they're not 'real' – a common complaint of people who have never read serious sci-fi. Sometimes she forgets she used to enjoy Jules Verne, but more of her literary tastes and the reasons for them later.

After further digging on the internet, I found a lithograph of the centre of Hradec Králové dating from 1900. It showed an attractive and wide town square with a fine Baroque Church near to a Gothic Cathedral. In the middle of the square stood the Plague Pillar, built in 1717 in gratitude to the Virgin Mary for the town's escape from the plague that had decimated central Europe the previous year. This university town was also home to Petrof Pianos, a company which would have still been active when Gustav lived there – and further internet browsing tells me that the town it is now famous for an annual hip-hop festival. I wonder what Gustav would have made of that. This sort of speculation can make the past feel a very long way away, but I've also discovered that the company that employed Gustav – *Českomoravská Kolben-Daněk* – has its own Facebook page today, so past and present collide after all.

Their Facebook page is, inevitably, written in Czech, and while I might know the Czech words for 'please', 'thank you' and 'dumplings' – the three most useful words in any central European language – that's as far as it goes. I have run into this problem time and time again during my researches. Google offers to 'translate this page' when it's in Czech, but rarely makes the offer for Slovak, and that's the language I've needed most. I don't speak a single word of Slovak and know nothing of its grammatical constructions. As my researches progressed, I discovered I was unable even to predict what a 'word' might be. Here's a typical example of the problem: Mother sent me the text of a poem she had recited in a school performance. I looked at the hand-written note and found it impossible to say with any confidence where any one word began or ended. When I phoned Mother and asked her to spell out each word in order to clarify matters, I learned that the letter 's' is a word in itself – a conjunction. No wonder I couldn't work it out.

Gustav's employer ČKD was a company which already had a long and illustrious history by the time he joined. It would have been easy for me to become sidetracked, but rather than delving into the various mergers before the thirties, I stuck to the company as it was when Gustav was managing their showroom in Bratislava in the 1930s. The translatable Czech references told me that he was one of around twelve thousand employees of ČKD across central Europe at that time. The company was, and still is, a major force in Czech engineering. Their slogan boasted that they made everything 'from pins to locomotives'. In the 1930s they were manufacturing a vast array of engineering equipment, from *Praga* automobiles, in direct competition with *Škoda*, to electrically-operated lifts and cranes – as well as domestic appliances such as washing machines and fridges.

Production inevitably came to a halt with the outbreak of the Second World War. I would later find out how Gustav lost his job because being an atheist was irrelevant if you were considered to be ethnically Jewish; the family as a consequence lost their home, and the factory left the locomotives and hydraulics equipment behind and started producing munitions for the German army. An allied air raid in 1945 put paid to all of this. The company gradually recovered, was nationalised and returned at last to civil engineering and tram-building, but this would all be too late for my grandfather.

Outside business hours, Gustav was a keen stamp collector, specialising in the stamps of the Austro-Hungarian Empire and early airmail covers. A favourite pastime was to meet with his fellow enthusiasts at a café after work to discuss all things philatelic. Quite apart from the chat and the opportunity for swapping stamps, the café meetings provided a welcome outlet for his smoking habit. He loved a cigar, but had strict rules about such things at home where he had always enforced a strict no-smoking regime in the belief that smoking in front of women was wrong. When Gustav's brother-in-law Otto, who was a heavy smoker, came to visit, the poor man had to be banished to the balcony to puff away – not to save the others from the dangers of passive smoking, but to protect them from witnessing this dangerously masculine habit.

One of the Gustav's stamp-collecting cronies was a man called Hugo Kaufmann, who ran a philately business. His daughter Gerda was to become one of Jana's best friends and the families became very close. I met Gerda and her mother Ilona as they visited us in England once when I was a child and we went for a stroll together through the Kentish countryside to visit the Wilberforce oak. I knew Gerda was an old friend of my mother's from Czechoslovakia, but that was all. I had no idea that the pleasant old lady, whom I knew as Mrs Kolar, was the Mrs Kaufmann who would feature at critical points throughout this story. I knew nothing about the times the Kaufmanns had lived through, or how the lives of Gerda and my mother were intertwined. I didn't even know about the stamp collecting. Now that I do, I like to picture Hugo Kaufmann and my grandfather, Gustav, sitting together in a café, drinking strong coffee and discussing all matters philatelic through a haze of cigar smoke. I've seen films of the café society of Vienna in the thirties, and I imagine Bratislava, just across the border in Slovakia, couldn't have been very different – same dirty old river, never as blue as in Strauss's eponymous waltz; the same cosmopolitan culture.

Gustav's career with ČKD had begun in Prague, but with promotion came the need to be transferred to different branches. At the start of WW1, he was working in Budapest with his first wife, Elsa. This is where the eldest of the children, his daughter Máňa was born. Elsa died aged thirty-six in 1924 when Máňa was just ten years old, but the little girl soon had a new step-mother in Kamila, who was Elsa's younger sister by three years.

After his stint in Budapest, Gustav was promoted to the post of branch manager of the ČKD showroom in Bratislava. By 1930, he and Kamila had two young sons, Jirka and Pavel, born in 1926 and 1928 respectively. Jana

21

was on the way, and would be born in August 1930. The family were now living in a comfortable and well-appointed apartment over the main company showroom in the heart of the vibrant and cultured city of Bratislava. Life was good for Gustav, whether at home, deciding where to display his latest artworks and ornaments, or in a café with his friends, enjoying a fine cigar and peering at the perforations on a recently acquired postage stamp.

This feels like a different world, especially since I've found out that the old ČKD showroom in Bratislava is now operating as a branch of TONI&GUY. However, I feel I 'know' Gustav a bit better now, so I'll move onto his second wife, my grandmother Kamila. Mother has far more information about her family, so this should be easier.

3

KAMILA

Mother may not have been able to tell me much about her father's early life, but both she and her brother Paul have been able to provide plenty of information about their mother, Kamila Gráfová, née Löwnerová. I've added the suffix *ová* to Kamila's surnames because *ová* means 'property of' and in Czech nomenclature the woman is always the property of the man – I'm squirming as I write this. She's the property of her father when young and of her husband after marriage. This system is still in use today, so I've stuck to it throughout the text however much it makes me want to gnaw the table.

Kamila was born in Lány, a village twenty-two miles west of Prague, just off the E48 Karlovy Vary road. Her father, Sigmund, was the village shopkeeper, and they lived above the shop on land that had once been part of the castle estate in the corner of the Křivoklát woods. Sigmund's shop was a general store selling everything from bread and milk to gardening tools – but not cheese. He drew the line at cheese, because he couldn't abide the smell. The shop had first come into the family when it was bought by Sigmund's father, Leopold in 1852. Before being a shop, the building had seen service as both a parsonage and a school. Leopold left the business to his eldest son, Adolf. As Adolf didn't have any children, it then passed to his surviving brother, Sigmund.

The shop was run on the 'small profit' method where large quantities of goods were sold with very narrow

23

profit margins. As a result, the family lived on a strict budget and finances were always tight. For example, on one occasion when the family was on holiday, the children – and it was a large family – had to divide a single orange between them.

Sigmund must have inherited the shop between 1888 and 1890, as that's when the records of place of birth for his children changes. Before moving to Lány, the family lived in a small town called Nové Strašecí, about five kilometres to the West of Lány. This is where Sigmund would eventually be buried, in the Jewish cemetery. Nové Strašecí – nicknamed 'New Bubu' – was a medieval town that was regularly razed to the ground by fires and warfare throughout its history. By the mid 1850s, however, things were looking up. Although it only had a population of 2200 at this point, a rail link to Prague was being built and it managed to support a fire brigade, a Reader's Club (1869), and a branch of the Youth Sports Association 'Sokol' (1869). I have no idea if Sigmund and his wife Johanna had anything to do with Sokol, but nearly eighty years later Jana, their granddaughter, would join a branch of the association in London.

The first of Kamila's brothers and sisters to be born in Nové Strašecí was Olga, who was either stillborn or died in infancy sometime in the mid 1880s. Next came Max, in 1887. He went on to obtain the same 'Ing' qualification as his future brother-in-law, Gustav, though he later became an architect. After Max came Elsa, born in 1888. She became Gustav's first wife, which is how their daughter Máňa was Jana's half sister. The family moved to Lány around this time. The first of the children to be born after the move was Viktor, in 1890. Next came Kamila, in 1891, Gustav's second wife and Jana's mother. Then there was another brother, Karel, in 1893. He went on to become a notable mathematician, and was one of the very few members of the family to survive the war as he and his wife Elizabeth managed to arrange passage to the United States early on, while such things were still possible. I have included

Elizabeth's account of their emigration in an appendix at the end of the book. Next came Terezie ('Aunt Rezi') in 1894, Milada in 1896, Otto – the chain-smoker who was banished to the balcony by Gustav – in 1899, and there may have been another daughter, who I assume died in infancy as there are no further records of her. Birth and death records are very hard to locate as so many were destroyed in the war.

The brothers and sisters were roped into shop-related duties as soon as they were old enough to make themselves useful. One chore was to wash the dried fruit that was earmarked for the chateau at Lány. Quite why the chateau staff couldn't do this task themselves remains a mystery, but perhaps 'pre-washed' dried fruit was a selling point, so this was good for business. Later on, Kamila was promoted from dried fruit washer to the somewhat more interesting task of buyer. She would take the train to Prague and visit various manufacturers and suppliers, most of whom were not at all impressed with having to deal with a woman, and even less with a slip of a girl. Kamila, however, was stubborn. She would wait for hours in reception, wearing them down with her presence until they finally gave in and felt obliged to see her, at which point her negotiating skills would enable her to buy whatever the shop required. I think my mother has inherited some of Kamila's stubbornness – as have I, no doubt.

Out of all her brothers and sisters, Kamila was closest to her brother Karel, probably because they were the middle two of a large family and only a couple of years apart in age. The future mathematician Karel was a keen chess player and already showed signs of an aptitude for working out complex problems. He would often lie on the floor with his eyes shut, and if asked to get up would say he couldn't because he was busy playing chess in his head. One day he and Kamila decided to write an opera together based on Friedrich Schiller's *The Robbers* (Die Reuber.) They made a start on the overture but quickly fell to arguing as to what it should represent or how to proceed. No further progress on this putative masterpiece was ever made, but the fact that they even thought of doing such a thing suggests this must have been a musical and cultured household.

Their father Sigmund was famous for his unique blend of coffee, so the shop naturally became the official coffee-supplier to the Lány chateau. When Count Fürstenburg, who owned the estate at the time, had to go away for any length of time he always instructed a servant to pick up his coffee supplies from Sigmund's shop. The special formula for the coffee blend was sadly lost when Sigmund died prematurely. He had suffered a mild stroke and gone to his doctor who advised him to take things easy and not return to work for some time. Sigmund became bored under this regime. He hated sitting around doing nothing, so he went back to work anyway. His doctor's warnings turned out to be justified – he suffered a more severe stroke soon afterwards which left him paralysed down one side. As a result, he had to stop working for good. He died not long after at the age of fifty-two.

With Sigmund gone, the family struggled to keep the shop going. It became increasingly difficult to make it pay. When it was losing too much money to remain viable, the decision was taken to sell up. The people who bought the shop must have had better business sense as they managed to make it a going concern once again. They briefly lost control under the Communist regime, but later restitution arrangements meant it eventually returned to their sole ownership.

I've never been to Lány, so I went back to Google maps to have a look. I typed in 'Lány', zoomed in on the map, picked a random point on a street, went to 'street view' and by pure chance found I'd landed directly opposite something calling itself a 'mini-market'; a smartly painted and fair-sized house that clearly contained a shop of some description on the ground floor plus living quarters upstairs. It could well have been the same place, as I knew the shop had been rebuilt in the 1930s, so I wasn't surprised to find it didn't look particularly old. To double-check, I rang up Mother. Yes, it had to be the same one – she had visited there many years later to see where her family came from, and could confirm its position in the south-west corner of the village. Having established the location, I took a virtual stroll along the street where my grandmother and her parents and grandparents must have walked many times. The gardens that front the smart neighbouring houses were full of fruit trees and the farmland on the edge of the village looked rich and fertile. I tried to turn down the road that led to the famous chateau, where they liked their dried fruit well washed and enjoyed a secret blend of coffee, but 'street view' wouldn't let me, so I researched the chateau the old-fashioned way.

Czech tourist sites are full of pictures of this imposing building, but apparently you can't visit it except on rare occasions. It's been the official summer residence of the Czech presidents for some years now, which no doubt accounts for my earlier difficulty when trying to saunter inconspicuously down the main drive. The earliest records I can find date from 1392, when the castle was a simple wooden keep, which will have borne scant resemblance to the increasingly complex baroque confection it became in the twentieth century.

Kamila's parents and grandparents may have been village shopkeepers, but she and her brothers and sisters were not destined to remain stock-takers and shelf-stackers. Sigmund and his wife Johanna were great believers in the German traditions of education, so although the brothers and sisters all attended the local Czech primary school, they followed this with a secondary education at a German-speaking Gymnasium – a grammar school equivalent – where they could gain a strong grounding in science, art, music and business. This style of cosmopolitan and multi-linguistic education was the norm during the final years of the Austro-Hungarian Empire and the high levels of education paid off for all the youngsters.

Kamila's eldest brother, Max, went on to become a well-known architect in Karlovy Vary, the elegant spa town in Western Bohemia, known in German as Carlsbad. Jana

27

thinks she met him when she was a small child, but has no clear memories, so suspects he didn't live in Prague, which is where they would often go to see other uncles and aunts. Max died before the war, shortly after marrying a Sudeten German called Giza. She was deported to Germany after the war despite Max's brother Viktor's efforts to help her to stay.

Another of Kamila's brothers, the chess-playing Karel, also left shop-keeping far behind and completed a doctorate in geometric function theory at Karlova (Charles) University in Prague. It was here that he first met Albert Einstein. The two would meet again at Berlin University, before both were forced to flee Europe for the United States. Karel later worked on the Manhattan Project, but like all the other mathematicians and physicists working on this at the time, he had no idea what the government's intentions were or to where this research would ultimately lead.

As for Kamila herself, after attending the Gymnasium along with her brothers and sisters, she completed her education at a business college. By the time she left, she spoke German fluently and had a good grasp of English. With these skills in hand, along with the business confidence she had gained as a buyer for her father's shop, she had no problem finding work as a secretary with an import/export firm where she dealt with clients' correspondence in Czech, German or English, as required.

A few years later, Kamila, the multi-lingual secretary, and Gustav, the artistically inclined engineer, would meet and marry and raise a family. Nothing so very extraordinary about that – except for the way their lives were about to be hi-jacked by world events.

4

THE FLAT ABOVE THE SHOWROOM

In 1930, Kamila was pregnant with her third child. The apartment where she and Gustav were living, though a good size, wasn't a mansion, but they would all squeeze in somehow. Gustav's sixteen year old daughter from his first marriage, Maria Veronica, known as Máňa, was already having to share her bedroom with her two little brothers – four year old Jiři, whose name was always shortened to Jirka, usually described as 'the grubby one'; and two year old Pavel, my 'Uncle Paul', known as 'the grizzly one'. In similar vein, when Jana arrived on the scene she would be known as 'the wet pants one' – in Czech it more or less rhymes, though as she grew older, she began to resent the nickname, reasonably enough.

Only Jirka, as Kamila's first baby, had been born in hospital. Pavel had been born in the apartment. After his birth, Kamila was warned not to have any more children for health reasons, but as she later told Jana, accidents will happen, and she became pregnant again. Her doctor advised her to have an abortion, but she refused. Luckily for all concerned, the pregnancy and birth were normal with no complications. The youngest member of the family, Jana, was born at home on the first of August, 1930, with Aunt Rézi (Kamila's younger sister Terezie) there to assist. The new baby was named 'Jana Anna' after Jana's two deceased grandmothers, Anna Gráfova and Johanna Löwnerova. Family, friends and school called Jana variously Hana,

Hanka, Hanička or Janka, but she generally refers to herself as 'Jana' so that's the name I'll use throughout this narrative.

The apartment above the showroom where Gustav was employed in the heart of Bratislava came rent-free with the job. The accommodation was spacious and well appointed, but as there were only two family-sized bedrooms, Jana had to sleep at first in a cot in her parents' room. When she had outgrown the cot, she joined her brothers and half-sister in the other bedroom. Both rooms had small tiled stoves for heating, but these were generally only lit if someone was ill. The apartment was well insulated and warm enough to rarely need this additional heating.

The entrance door to the apartment opened onto a spacious hallway which the younger children utilised to ride their tricycles when the weather was too bad to go outside. If you could ride a trike up and down, it must have been a fair size. That certainly wouldn't have been possible in the house where I grew up.

The doors from the hallway opened into the two main reception rooms. The dining room table was large enough for games of table tennis or table croquet. It also contained a coke-fuelled 'American' style stove which warmed the entire flat when the doors were left open. This would be lit continuously from autumn to spring, and was no doubt necessary as the average winter temperature in Bratislava is -2° C, dropping to around -5° in January. When the weather was especially cold, Jana sat in front of the stove and liked to watch the glowing fire through its mica panels. The entire flat was double-glazed, which in combination with the efficient stove meant the place was snug throughout the winter.

A baby-grand piano had pride of place in the lounge and was much used. The kitchen housed a wood-burning Aga-style range for heating water and cooking, and there was also a gas cooker which ran on mains gas. Just off the kitchen was a small additional bedroom for a live-in maid to use.

All the walls were distempered except for one room which had patterned walls; painted with a stencil to imitate wallpaper. Jana didn't know such a thing as wallpaper existed until she visited a school friend's house a few years later where all the walls were papered. When she told her mother about this, Kamila explained it was a very old-fashioned way of decorating.

The bathroom had a gas-fired geyser for instant hot water and a hand held shower attachment over the bath, which was very unusual in those days.

There was plenty of space for the washing machine. Occasionally Gustav brought domestic appliances home from work for Kamila to try out. She was not impressed with the fridge, and sent it back, but she loved the washing machine prototype and kept it despite its habit of dancing across the floor when spinning.

An additional small windowless box room was used by Kamila as a dark room to indulge her passion for photography. She used an Agfa camera – I don't know which model, but I've seen some of the photos.

The flat had three balconies: two to the front with views of the National Theatre and its surrounding park, and one off the hall to the back, overlooking the courtyard and garages. The flats are still there, as is the old theatre, though there is now a new National Theatre complex in another part of the city. The clue to the relatively luxury of the flat was its location. This was not the 'flat over the shop'; this was the branch manager's comfortable apartment above a large showroom opposite a beautiful theatre that resembled the Paris Opera House in style, if not scale.

Hviezdoslavovo Námestie – the paved square in front of the theatre – was used for political rallies. During one such rally, when the speaker called for Slovak autonomy, someone in the crowd shouted back, 'We don't want auto-wotsits – we've got horses!' It probably sounds better in Slovak. Mother has flagged up what she finds funny in the notes she's sent me by use of exclamation marks but I guess you had to be there. Political rallies aside, the park opposite the flat was the place to play. This was the preferred race track for the children's tricycles in fine weather, though they had to be careful to keep off the formal lawns and avoid veering into the ornamental flowerbeds or bumping into the chestnut trees. Nowadays the square has wide, attractive cobbled areas and not so many lawns, but there are still plenty of trees, including chestnuts.

I've just re-read the description of the apartment and can't help but compare it with my own modest childhood home. When I grew up in the sixties in a comfortable enough semi-detached house in Greater London, we certainly didn't have the luxury of double-glazing, though my father did eventually fit some rudimentary secondary glazing. Those were the days of fascinating ice-crystal patterns on the inside of your bedroom window in winter. We had no central heating at first, and wouldn't have dreamt of opening all the interior doors to spread what little heat there was around the house. A special treat if it was really cold would be to have a hot water bottle plus the portable Baby Belling electric fire on for an hour in your bedroom before you went to bed. I have no idea how much power that little heater must have used, but I still love the smell of burning dust as I associate it with rare winter warmth.

My mother's first washing machine was a basic single tub affair with a wringer on top, though she later had a series of little spin dryers that waltzed across the floor and no doubt brought back memories of Kamila's prototype. Our piano was a modest upright, there being no space for a baby grand even if we could have afforded one. My father played all his life, and my brother and I both had piano lessons as children, following on the family tradition. Dad loved his photography, but there was no spare room to be used as a darkroom until both my brother and I had left home, at which point my old room became a utility room and my brother's an 'everything else' room.

I never realised until my mother sent me notes about her apartment that her original home had a room for a live-in maid. I wonder what this maid did in the Graf household, and whether 'maid' is even the right word, with its connotations of stately homes and young women in service. I suspected 'mother's help' might be closer.

I phoned Mother to ask about the maid/mother's help/skivvy/cook/*au pair* or whatever she was who slept in the small room off the kitchen. Apparently it was customary for town ladies to take a country girl in as a maid and train her up in cookery and general household management. This all sounds a bit Mrs Beeton to me. The family had a number of these maids. They changed frequently and it seems were not especially memorable except for the last one, a girl called Anna, who was, as Mother put it, 'mentally peculiar' so had to be sent home. When pushed for particulars, Mother says as far as she can recall the poor girl had a persecution complex and limited understanding.

I wonder what became of poor Anna.

I grew up in the sixties on hearty breakfasts of cereal, eggs, bacon, tomatoes, fried bread, toast and marmalade, with chocolate flavoured Nesquik to drink; but Jana's childhood breakfasts were much lighter and would typically comprise rolls and butter, with coffee for the adults and milk or chocolate for the children. As they grew older, the children graduated onto milky coffee, which no doubt grew stronger as time went on. Since adulthood, my mother has subsisted on what I consider to be viciously strong black coffee drunk in copious quantities. I went through a brief black coffee phase, just to see what it's like. I didn't keep it up for very long.

Lunch was the main meal of the day when my mother was growing up. The first course would be soup, either a homemade vegetable soup, or a beef broth made from the stock the beef had been boiled in for the main course. On broth days the boiled beef would be served with a tomato, dill, mushroom or mustard sauce, and of course there would be *knedliky* (dumplings). A slight digression here, but the best thing about having a Czech mother when you're growing up is eating knedliky, ideally served with pot-roasted brisket and vegetable marrow in a dill sauce. I'm salivating just thinking about it. I'll put a few recipes at the end of the book for anyone interested in having a go at making this. If you hunt for it on YouTube, you may be lucky enough to find the delightful video of a ninety-five year old Czech lady showing us how to make these exquisite dumplings. I don't know who she is, but she has my mother's way of speaking – not the accent so much as the way she says things, showing that people who learn second languages often can't help but retain the inflexions and underlying grammar of their mother tongue, however fluent they become.

But I digress. On the non-broth days, the main course would be other roast meats, goulash, or schnitzel, with roast chicken or duck on Sundays. Brussels sprouts were the only plain boiled vegetables. Everything else would be stewed or braised in butter with various additions such as caraway seed for white cabbage; apple, spices, sugar and vinegar for red cabbage, and so on. A typical dessert would be fruit or jam dumplings, or stewed or bottled fruit. Trifle would sometimes be served as a special treat.

The next meal of the day was a sort of light afternoon tea to keep you going until supper. This tea meal consisted of coffee or milk, and cake, which might be a fruit flan made from yeast dough, or *buchty* – another of those delicious Czech recipes, like the knedliky, which makes me yearn to stop writing and get my hands floury.

Supper might be open sandwiches or recycled leftovers from lunch. Knedliky might be cut up into chunks and served fried with scrambled eggs. I used to wolf down this dish during my own childhood. It doesn't sound particularly appetising, but it was delicious. The whole 'supper' meal sounds much like the 'tea' meal I used to enjoy on Sundays evenings after an afternoon's country walking.

For their birthdays, the children were allowed to choose their own menus. Jana's choice was always tomato soup, followed by *Wiener Schnitzel* with new potatoes and dressed lettuce, finishing with apricot dumplings for dessert. I'd happily eat all of that, though I'd swap the apricots for cherries or plums. Again, 'fruit dumplings' sounds a little dull but they're not: you need to imagine whole fruits wrapped in a light and fragrant dough made from curd cheese, simmered gently till cooked, then cut open so that the fruit bursts out; all served with a drizzle of sizzling hot melted butter and a generous sprinkling of sugar and cinnamon. Nothing dull about that.

Once a month, the whole family went out for a meal in a restaurant about ten minutes' walk from the flat. The restaurant, called *Reduta*, has since been converted to a concert hall. I've had a look at it online and it looks to be a sumptuous and elegant baroque style building. The main purpose of going out for a meal was to teach the children the correct way to behave in company. They were allowed to choose anything from the menu. Jana would pick whatever she fancied at the time, but her brother Jirka always ordered the most expensive dishes like asparagus and smoked salmon, simply because they *were* the most expensive, and he was like that.

When I was little, we occasionally went as a family into tea shops as a treat on summer holidays at the seaside, and we would sometimes stop at grim motorway service stations, but restaurants? Never. Quite apart from the expense, I very much doubt if children were made welcome in restaurants in England in the sixties. This was before the invention of the child-friendly pub lunch, so theoretically, I've never learnt how to behave properly in a restaurant. I feel so uncouth all of a sudden. These Austro-Hungarian children had a sophistication I and my peers would never know. I used to take my own children regularly to a certain well-known fast food emporium, to my eternal shame – but at least I knew they wouldn't be kicked out for failing to use the cutlery correctly, as there wasn't any.

5

DIE SCHÖNE MÜLLERIN

I've asked Mother to tell me her very earliest memories. She's sent me a note in reply in which she describes trying to stay upright on her parents' bed on a Sunday morning while everyone else shook the mattress and counted to see how long it would take her to topple. I imagine she can't have been more than about two years old at the time. On other occasions, her father, Gustav, would lie across the bed and try to lift her up with his feet. I used to indulge in this sort of rough and tumble play with my own children when they were tiny, especially with the eldest, who loved it all, but I have no recollection of my parents ever doing anything similar with me. Perhaps they did and I've forgotten, or perhaps this type of play skipped a generation for some reason – the flipside of the 'swinging sixties' may have been a sense of propriety in English lower middle class families that bore little relation to the more relaxed culture of family life in central Europe between the wars.

The Sunday morning gymnastics on her parents' bed were followed by marginally more sophisticated exercises. The top jamb of the door between the dining room and the children's bedroom had two hooks from which a swing, rings or a trapeze could be hung. This set the tone for Jana's enthusiasm for all things gymnastic that was to last for years. Even now, it's probably her favourite sport (after tennis) to watch on the television.

Aside from the proto-gymnastics, her other very early memory is of her mother, Kamila, singing Schubert

Lieder to her, at a time when other children would be listening to traditional nursery rhymes. The favourites were *Die Schöne Müllerin* and *Die Forelle*. Kamila wasn't a professional singer, but she came from a family where everybody learnt an instrument as a matter of course. She could play the piano, but preferred to sing. This early exposure to art music had a profound effect on the whole family. Jana became a lifelong devotee of classical music, particularly opera, and ended up marrying my father who played the piano practically every day of his life, apart from an enforced break during the war when he was stationed, minus piano, in Ghana.

Jana's sister, Máňa, continued the musical tradition by playing the piano and marrying the renowned opera singer, Otakar Kraus. Their son, my cousin Charles, would later work for the management of English National Opera and their grandson, Tony, conducts for Opera North. I'm not suggesting that if you sing Schubert to your children, they will automatically marry musicians and produce musical dynasties, but there has to be an effect on the developing brain of hearing classical music continuously as an infant. I grew up listening to my dad playing Chopin and Beethoven as I was falling asleep every night, and ended up training as a professional classical musician. I even married a fellow classical musician – though we've since divorced and I've married a non-musician, thus proving escape is possible.

Gustav was more into folk music than classical, and would sing traditional ballads to the children rather than *Lieder*. This is a relief, frankly. You can overdose on the highbrow. I grew up on a strict diet of BBC Radio Three at home, but despite this, one of the first LPs I ever bought was Pink Floyd's *Dark Side of the Moon*, and I've idolised David Bowie all my life. I suspect I might have admired Kamila's lovely singing, but secretly been more interested in Gustav's folk repertoire. The folk music did stick in Jana's memory, however, despite the heavy doses of Schubert. When I was about seven years old, we had a family seaside holiday in a cottage near Tenby, on the Pembrokeshire coast in South

Wales. Máňa joined us that particular year. One of my most vivid memories is walking along the footpath to Amroth with my mother and Máňa singing the folk songs they used to sing as children while the rest of us gathered blackberries – and I looked forward to a rum and raisin ice cream at the end of the walk. I'm positive they didn't sing any Schubert. The folk songs stayed in my mind so clearly that later at music college I made settings of them for soprano and piano and even had the pieces performed. Nowadays I prefer raw folk music to the sort of sanitised classical arrangement I made back then. I have heard recordings of Máňa's husband Otto singing this sort of 'art music' arrangement of the folk repertoire, and whilst his voice is glorious, the treatment of the music makes me wince.

Having the National Theatre just across the park from the flat reinforced the normality of classical vocal music for the children as the theatre routinely put on Sunday matinees of operas and operettas suitable for youngsters. Jana saw Bedřich Smetana's *The Bartered Bride* there when she was just six years old. This was her first experience of opera, and she never looked back. I can understand why she was so taken with this particular work. When I was small, we had an EP of the overture, polka and furiant from *The Bartered Bride*, and I found the pieces utterly engaging and played the record often. That love of opera has never faded for either of us, even if our tastes rarely coincide entirely. Even today Jana regularly treks up to London to watch dress rehearsals of English National Opera's latest productions. In a similar way, I was taken to see Benjamin Britten's more child-friendly operas as a youngster, and graduated to regular trips to English National Opera for the heavier fare. After one performance of *Cavalleria Rusticana* and *Pagliacci* I thought, 'I want to do that; I want to be playing in the pit orchestra'. It happened; I did it, I achieved my ambition and played for many operas, including *Cav* and *Pag*. Was I living out my mother's frustrated musical ambitions? To a certain extent, perhaps I was, but I enjoyed myself anyway. However, despite my profession as a classical musician, if I'm going to listen to live music nowadays, my preference is for prog rock or rock-blues, with a bit of metal thrown in, but I'd best not mention that, or the fact that Schubert *Lieder* is the last thing I'd ever listen to, given the choice. At least I still enjoy opera.

In the Graf household, Kamila was the great opera lover. She had a subscription to all the productions at the National Theatre, and Gustav loyally accompanied her, but opera wasn't really his thing. He became famous in the family for managing to sleep pretty much all the way through Wagner's *Parsifal*, one of the longest operas in the repertoire. I could never sleep through Wagner, but I love that my maverick grandfather did.

The children were given every encouragement musically. Máňa was an able pianist and studied theory and harmony at a music school. Jirka was very gifted both academically and musically, going to secondary school a year early, where he amazed everyone with his piano playing. Jana says that Pavel was jealous of Jirka's talents, though I would imagine he would deny this. Pavel grew up to be a highly gifted mathematician, so it follows that he must have been a clever child, but presumably in Jana's eyes, here elder brother was the one who shone. He would never be a threat to her own abilities because he was so much older, but Pavel was closer in age, so sibling rivalry between the boys set in early on.

Pavel and Jana both started piano lessons in 1938, when Jana was eight and Pavel ten. Their teacher said that Pavel played with great accuracy but little expression; and Jana with plenty of feeling but the wrong notes. Having heard my mother sing, I suspect she may have been playing more or less the right notes, perhaps even in approximately the right order – but at the wrong time. A sense of rhythm has never been her strong point. Pavel ended up working full time for IBM, so I'm confident his grasp of rhythmic patterns was more sophisticated. I can't know how Jirka played, but if he combined Pavel's accuracy and instinct for mathematical patterns with Jana's expressive abilities, he probably outshone them both with ease.

The eventual coming of war would mean the loss of the piano and the end of music lessons. Jana never attempted to learn any instrument again. Instead, she became a lifelong devotee of opera as a listener rather than a performer, but she still sings to herself with a delightful inaccuracy and trademark inattention to where the beat really comes – and she'll probably throw this book at me when she reads that comment, especially as she's always loved to dance, so of *course* she must have a great sense of rhythm.

6

HERMA THE SEAMSTRESS

The other children living in the block of flats were all boys, so until Jana started nursery school aged four and a half she hadn't played with any other girls. This contrasts with my own childhood, where I had both girls and boys close to my own age as neighbours, and also attended a mixed nursery school followed by mixed primary school, so had the best of both worlds. Jana's early experience of only having boys to play with may be one of the reasons why when she eventually found girls of her own age, she was so keen to join in their activities and leave the boyish games behind, whereas I wasn't so interested in the girly stuff, having had plenty of it when I was very small.

One of Jana's earliest playmates in the flats was a little boy of her own age called Ivan Čermák. Jirka was friends with Ivan's older brother, Fedor. The Čermák brothers were the sons of one of Gustav's colleagues and lived on the floor above the Graf family. Jana's brother Pavel was less gregarious than his siblings, but had a playmate of his own age in Vláďa Rybák, the son of the company's accountant. The Čermáks were Slovak, but Vláďa was Czech, so in the way of children in similar situations the world over, the children grew up bilingual, switching easily from Czech to Slovak and back again as required. Jana's parents spoke only Czech, but they understood Slovak well enough to get by. This would be an essential language for Jana later on, as it was the only language spoken at school. Despite being born in Slovakia, spending her entire childhood and early teens there, never living in what is now the Czech Republic, and speaking Slovak with complete fluency from a very young age, Jana still considers herself Czech, rather than Slovak, as her parents were Czech. This was something I could never understand as a child, but I've since grown to appreciate why my mother chose the previous generation's nationality, irrespective of her own geographical upbringing. I, on the other hand, have always considered myself 100% English, despite having a Czech mother. As I grew up I was vaguely proud of having a 'foreign' mother, and felt it gave me some kudos at school, but that was as far as it went – but I grew up in a time of stability, with parents that spoke the language I heard at school, and that has to make a huge difference to how one sees one's national identity.

Jana didn't have any specific toys of her own at first, so she and Ivan Čermák played with building bricks and other construction toys, along with the usual trains and cars. Fedor, being four years older, hung around more with Jirka and Pavel, so Jana had little to do with him. Pavel's friend Vláďa always seemed too noisy and rough to her, so she didn't like to play with him or any other older boys indoors, but outside was another matter. All the children would play together in either the Graf's or the Čermák's garden. I'm sure this is often the way. Thinking back, although I would play with my brother indoors, it was mostly outside that I would play with the neighbouring boys – indoors would be girls only. For Jana and her brothers and friends, the favourite outdoor games were the universal ones of climbing trees, blind man's buff, and hide and seek. There were also variations on 'catch'. In one, the child who was 'it' would stand in the middle while everyone else stood next to a tree. The idea was to swap trees without the child in the middle being able to reach your tree first. If they did, you became 'it' and had to stand in the middle. Another game, 'Golden Gate', had actions similar to the 'Here is the chopper to chop off your head' part of 'Oranges and Lemons'. There was a song to accompany this game, which included the phrase *zlátá brána* (golden arch or golden gate). Researching the game, I found that the phrase was used as the name of a Czech children's television series in the seventies and eighties, so I would guess the game was as popular and well known as the English version.

As the younger sister of two brothers, it was inevitable that Jana's earliest toys were hand-me-down trains and cars. At first she didn't know these were traditional boys' toys as she wasn't mixing with girls, and the other boys in the block didn't own or want to play with dolls anyway. I would have been delighted with the situation, as I was always jealous of my brother's toys, particularly decent construction toys like Meccano. Girls weren't expected to play with such things back then, as the instruction booklets and boxes of the time made clear with their illustrations of earnest and enthusiastic boys and pipe-smoking fathers looking on encouragingly (I may be imagining the latter). I was recently sorting out my attic and found the instruction booklet for an 'Erector' set (a predecessor of Meccano, first produced in 1913) which includes a sentence telling me what a lucky boy I am to own this toy. This is what I was always up against as a child. Yes, I enjoyed my toy farm, my garden set and my dolls' house and was very fond of my soft toys, but I would have loved a decent train set. Were the sixties in England an inherently more sexist time for children than the thirties in Slovakia? Very hard to know at this distance, but these things go in cycles. The girls' aisles in toyshops today are virulently pink in a way they never were in my childhood. We seem to be going backwards.

Gender politics aside, I'm sure Jana was much more a doll person than I ever been; far more of a girly girl despite only having boys to play with when she was very small. I dutifully dressed my Sindy in her classic jeans and stripy top, but I preferred my tough little plastic crocodile. Jana, on the other hand, wanted dolls as soon as she was old enough to realise such things existed, and eventually she got them.

Aunt Herma (Hermine/Wilhelmina) was Gustav's elder sister by three years. She lived in Vienna with her twin sons, Gusti (Gustav) and Dolfi (Adolf). The boys were a little older than Máňa – they're the ones who took her to a political meeting in Vienna when she wanted to go shopping. Jana has few memories of these visits to Vienna in the early thirties, other than going to the Prater, the historic funfair that still draws crowds today. As Gusti and Dolfi were Máňa's contemporaries, Jana had little to do with them and certainly wouldn't have played with them. She adored her Aunt Herma, and I'm sure the feeling was mutual, as according to Kamila, Herma had longed to have a daughter herself. After having the twin boys, she had another set of twins, a boy and a girl, but sadly they only survived a few days, and she didn't have any further children.

The usual pattern on these visits to Vienna would be for Kamila to take the youngsters to the Prater while Gustav stayed behind to chat with his sister. At first the family travelled to Vienna by tram, a distance of around 79km, but when that service was discontinued they had to find some other means of transport. The family had use of a company car, which they shared with the Čermáks. Gustav and Kamila didn't drive, so the porter in the apartment block, Mr Muzikář, would chauffeur them. The trips were co-ordinated with the Čermák family so that the two families wouldn't want the car at the same time.

Visiting Aunt Herma meant crossing the border from Slovakia into Austria, and there were rules about how much cash you could be carrying. Pavel has told me how the family would take more money than was allowed, and Mr Muzikář would hide the excess in his jacket pocket. When the border guards asked about money, he would open his jacket and say, 'See, there's no money!' and the border guards would believe him, say 'Okay', and let them through. Such easy-going border controls would soon be a thing of the past, but in the early thirties there were no problems.

Vienna itself wasn't the only destination on these trips. Sometimes the family went on to Klosterneuburg, about twenty minutes' drive north of Vienna on the Danube, to visit other relatives. These were Kamila's uncle and aunt, Marie Kraus and her husband, Ludwig, who was unrelated but had the same surname. Marie could speak Czech but the rest of the family were German speakers. They lived in a village house with an adjacent garden. At this point, all of Jana's friends lived in flats, so she found the house novel, but has no further memories of these visits. The family had two children. Years later, their son Georg moved to France where he changed his name to Georges. He lived in Grenoble and visited London after the war, the only time Jana met him, but as he spoke only German and French they weren't able to converse much. Jana had only the most rudimentary German and no French at all. His sister Marta hoped to have a career in films, but according to Kamila, this came to nothing as she refused to sleep with the producers. She later moved to Switzerland where she lived with her husband, Camillo Adler, though Jana doesn't think she ever met them. Records show that Georg and Marta's parents, Maria and Ludwig Kraus were deported on 14th July, 1942 and sent on transport 31-631 to the ghetto on Theresienstadt. On 21st September, 1942 they were sent on the transport Bp-523 to Treblinka death camp, where they were killed, probably two days later.

Klosterneuburg to Treblinka – it was hard to get my head round this sort of thing, but as I wrote this biography and became closer to so many people I could never meet, I had to steel myself and accept I would discover facts like this more and more often. My mother lived through all of this. I had to keep reminding myself that the little girl of these early chapters had all of this to come, and to survive, somehow.

One Christmas Aunt Herma came to stay in Bratislava, bringing proper girly presents at last for Jana. Herma had been widowed some years earlier so had given up work as a librarian to become a dressmaker, this being an occupation that fitted in more easily around bringing up her twin boys.

Herma the seamstress, with her professional skills, would naturally have been able to make exquisite dolls' clothes. The two dolls that Jana received stood just over a foot tall and had real hair, one short, the other long. Herma dressed them as boy and girl twins and provided several changes of outfits. The dolls were even treated to professional hairstyling. In the passageway between the street and the courtyard in the flats in Bratislava there was a short row of shops, one of which was a hairdresser's. When Jana went in for a haircut, she always took her dolls with her and the hairdressers curled their hair while Jana had a trim.

As the children grew older, their toys became more sophisticated. Kamila was fond of handicrafts and constructed a marionette theatre complete with changes of scenery. For several years, the children received new marionettes and other accessories for Christmas and birthday presents. I'm having visions of that dreadful little goatherd marionette in my least favourite scene from *The Sound of Music*. As this was happening at precisely the same period in a neighbouring country, perhaps that's not too far-fetched – though I doubt if Kamila ever indulged in any Julie Andrews-style yodelling. All the children were keen on playing with their puppet theatre, and would put on performances with their marionettes. Sometimes these were entirely made up, but sometimes they were actual puppet plays which you could buy in pamphlet form. Their regular playmates, Ivan, Fedor and Vláďa often joined in.

Other objects around the flat also became playthings. Gustav's collection of china figurines was put to good use. Jana liked to make up stories about these tiny people and choreograph stately dances for them around the dining room table. It would never have occurred to me to choreograph dances for my toys, though it should have done, as I had ballet lessons from the age of three. My toy farm had plenty of animals, so perhaps that was my equivalent, but the cows and pigs – along with the crocodile and brontosaurus – on my farm never danced. This was probably all for the best. I only have to look at a piece of porcelain and it cracks. I still have my collection of tiny china and glass figures from my own childhood, but they're all chipped. I doubt if Gustav would have allowed Jana to play with his precious collection if she'd been as clumsy as I am.

Siblings fight. If it's just one boy and one girl, they'll fight each other, as I know from my own experience, but if it's two boys and one girl, then it's more likely to be the brothers beating each other up. Jana has clear memories of Pavel and Jirka arguing and coming to blows. The younger brother, Pavel, was always at a disadvantage due to being that much smaller, so would vent his frustrations on his little sister. Jirka would feel honour bound to defend Jana, so Pavel would be on the receiving end again and would no doubt retaliate, would be yet again frustrated by his older brother's greater size and strength, so would turn on Jana again – and so it would go on. No wonder he tended to be a bit of a loner, with no one to take his side in these sibling battles. Playing by himself must have seemed like the safer option.

Sometimes you need a time out from battling brothers. For Jana, this happened on Sundays when Gustav would often take her for a stroll along the banks of the Danube. This was no energetic hiking exercise in hobnailed boots with rousing songs and knapsacks on their backs – just a little girl and her dad watching the boats on the river. Jana had her father's undivided attention on these occasions and loved it. They'd stand together watching the paddle steamer ferrying passengers across to the opposite bank, while a multitude of boats of all shapes and sizes steamed up and down river and other heavier ships passed by, carrying their cargo all the way from the wharves upstream down to the mouth of the Danube at the Black Sea.

Apart from these strolls along the river, Gustav had little interest in any physical activities. Kamila, by contrast, was keen walker and strong swimmer. She'd enjoyed walking with her friends in the woods and fields of Lány in her youth, and now took the children for walks at every opportunity. The same thing happened when I was small, but with me it was both parents who were keen walkers. I grew up thinking everyone – and I mean *everyone*, young and old – went for a family walk on a Sunday afternoon. I was shocked when I discovered I was the only one of my school mates who did this. I couldn't imagine what they must do with their time. What else was there to do on a Sunday afternoon? My mother still walks as often as she can and has been a member of various rambling clubs all her adult life. On one memorable occasion a photograph appeared on the front page of *The Times* showing my parents shortly after they'd become engaged leading the Morley College Rambling Club past the Gothic tower on Leith Hill in Surrey. How that photo came to be published is a mini-story in itself, as neither of my parents was particularly newsworthy – certainly not front-page-of-The-Times newsworthy – but it makes a wonderful memento of a lifelong enthusiasm for rambling, which for Jana started with her mother's own love of the outdoors. It's clear to me now that the foraging I've always done as a matter of course for berries and mushrooms when I am out in the countryside comes in a direct line from my grandmother, Kamila.

7

THE GARDEN IN NIGHTINGALE VALLEY

Jana was taken swimming before she could walk. She must have enjoyed this sort of activity because just before her fifth birthday, Kamila enrolled her in a music and movement class which included swimming with its weekly programme of exercises to music, as well as tap dancing. I've no idea if I would have liked swimming at such an early age as there was no opportunity to find out. The idea of babies in public swimming pools had yet to take off in England when I was an infant. I did, however, start ballet lessons at age three on the advice of the family doctor who thought it might cure my flat feet. It didn't, but like my mother before me, I learnt to love dancing and have done ever since.

During the summer months, Kamila took Jana and her brothers across the Danube to the Petržalka meadows to enjoy a picnic and fly their kites. The meadows were an idyllic wide grassy area with a pond and masses of wild flowers: oxeye daisies and buttercups, plus others that Jana couldn't name. Many other Bratislava families crossed the river to the meadows for summer picnics and kite flying. The usual way of getting there was via the one bridge that crossed the Danube at that time, though the far bank could also be reached by paddle steamer ferry.

The porter and occasional chauffeur, Mr Muzikář, was an experienced kite builder, so was on hand to help the children as they created ever more complex designs. He had a keen apprentice in Jirka especially. Kamila's handicraft skills were also in demand for kite construction, so eventually the children amassed an impressive collection of all different types.

I've looked in vain online for old photos of the meadows. If Kamila took any, they haven't survived. I did find a reference online to the Petržalka Lido, which was certainly in existence a decade or so earlier, and would still have been there when Jana and family visited. The water in the Lido, fed by the Danube, was icy cold for swimming, but the meadows did have their own pond, where Jana liked to sit and watch the frogs. She wasn't so happy when older brother Jirka – always the prankster – dropped a tiny frog down her neck. Years later, I used to be fascinated by the frogs in our neighbours' garden pond. My brother never tried to drop one down my neck, luckily for both of us, and I kept well clear when the neighbouring boys lined up the frogs for the annual 'races' that took place when the pond was drained for cleaning.

The Petržalka meadows are long gone; victims to housing development, though the outskirts of the Petržalka district still contains gardens and old trees. One bridge was never going to be enough for a city like Bratislava. A new one would inevitably be built, but unfortunately the new bridge construction destroyed much of the historic Jewish quarter. I've seen film clips of the lovely old buildings next to the river being knocked down in order to build the access roads. There were even plans at one point to knock down Bratislava's ancient castle, which had been a burnt out shell since a fire in 1811. The idea was to raze it to the ground and replace it with modern university buildings. Luckily there was a sufficient public outcry to prevent this happening and a full restoration programme finally got under way in 1957. Bratislava would have been a much poorer place without the distinctive upturned bedstead-shaped castle which had dominated the skyline for so long.

To break up the long summer holidays and get them out of the city, the family often rented a country cottage for a month or so in the foothills of the Tatras, most often in the village of Štóla in the Presov region of Northern Slovakia. Here they would indulge in their favourite pastimes of hiking, bilberry picking, and mushrooming. On one occasion when out walking, Jana nearly trod on an adder. Kamila pulled her away just in time, but the shock made a deep impression and she has been afraid of snakes ever since.

Gustav joined them for a week on some occasions, or just for the a weekend. As he was never a keen walker, he preferred to stay near the cottage, perhaps sitting out in the sun and having a quiet smoke of his favourite cigars while the family was off being energetic. Jana thinks he may have found other kindred spirits to join him in a hand of cards. When he had to return to the apartment in Bratislava on his own, his meals would be prepared by the maid, so he managed well enough.

This sort of self-catering holiday also informed my own childhood. Whitsun and summer were the times for a cottage in Wales or the West Country, scrambling up and down moors and mountains, picking bilberries and looking out for mushrooms. I assumed everyone did this. I had no idea my friends at school didn't spend their holidays on bracing country walks, carrying thermos flasks and scotch eggs. Even now I find it a bit strange that my husband likes to sunbathe by a hotel pool and rather than climb the nearest vertical peak. He is also perturbed if he sees me eating anything growing wild in a hedgerow. What if a dog has lifted its leg anywhere in the vicinity? As my wild foraging nowadays is mostly confined to picking raspberries off five foot high canes in Hamsterley Forest, I don't think there's much chance of that.

The family had just one seaside holiday, to the island of Krk, off the coast of Croatia, probably in 1933, when Jana was only three years old. On this occasion, unusually, they stayed in a hotel rather than a cottage. Her memories must be sketchy as she was so young at the time, but this holiday was very different to the usual hiking ones, so has remained surprisingly vivid. As she had been a water-baby since infancy, this was heaven for Jana. She had an inflatable crocodile to help her to swim, but what most impressed her was being allowed ice cream every day. These things matter when you're three – and when you're older, as my memories of rum and raisin ice cream during my seaside holiday near Tenby prove.

The family owned a garden-cum-allotment a short bus ride away from the apartment at a place called Slávičie Údolie, which translates as Nightingale Valley. Mr Muzikář's daughter Jiřina, who was about Máňa's age, sometimes accompanied them on visits here. I doubt if this was to dig the borders or spread manure. It wasn't that sort of a garden, but more of a mini-orchard, with soft fruit, cherry trees, apples, apricots, and a walnut tree. There was even a small olive tree, though it never produced any fruit. Kamila tried every so often to grow vegetables, but whatever she sowed always turned mysteriously into horseradish.

The summerhouse in the garden was mostly used as a shed for storing garden tools. I've seen photos of the building; a substantial timber construction on a sturdy stone built base. The rudimentary plumbing meant there was a water tap halfway down the garden, but there were no cooking facilities and if you needed the toilet you had to use the bushes at the far end. Some time just before the war, three young men, who Jana thinks had escaped from Bohemia (then the Protectorate) spent a few weeks in the summerhouse while waiting for their transport across Hungary and through Turkey to Palestine. Gustav and Kamila provided them with blankets and food, probably an oil lamp, and an oil cooking ring. These men weren't relations of the family, or known personally to them in any way, but a Jewish organisation had appealed for help and Gustav and Kamila were happy to oblige.

I think my mother must have inherited Kamila's not-so-green fingers. She loves fresh apples and cherries from the trees in the garden, but my father was always the gardener when I was growing up. We had fruit, vegetables, herbs and flowers in abundance – but not one horseradish plant. Mother is able to operate the lawnmower, but that's about it. There was no lawnmower at Nightingale Valley, so whenever the grass grew too tall the family borrowed a couple of goats from a local farmer to give it a trim. The garden contained a mulberry tree, but Jana didn't care much for its fruit. She liked pretty much everything else, which would in due course be harvested to be bottled or turned into jam.

Late summer and early autumn in my own childhood was also full of the aromas and bright red splashes of fruit being bottled and preserved. It was only later I discovered that some children had mothers who not only didn't do this, they probably didn't know how to make jam in the first place. If they ate preserved fruit, it would be a tin of peaches from the Co-op rather than home bottled cherries from a Kilner jar. My friends would have recognised a cherry but not a bilberry, as 'blueberries' weren't sold in the local greengrocer's in those days. The vast majority of my young friends had certainly never gone bilberrying, blackberrying or mushrooming. All toadstools were viewed with hostility, not only by my school friends, but pretty much anyone else. Mushrooms came in tins, or possibly in a punnet from the greengrocer's. Pick one from a field, and you would die in horrible agony. I've always accepted this as a real possibility, so since childhood I've only collect the varieties of mushrooms I've seen my mother pick, none of which look remotely like a Death Cap. My mother's old friend, Míla Stein, knew more than anyone about which varieties were good to eat, and I have clear memories of going with Míla onto Hayes Common to pick all kinds for us to eat later for supper. I always accepted Míla as the lady with the strong foreign accent who had the nice flat in London and who sometimes came down to see us and pick mushrooms – it wasn't until writing this biography that I discovered some of her background. She will reappear later in this story.

Despite my expertise at identifying good edible mushrooms, unfortunately I've never much liked the taste or even the thought of them. I still cook the wild-gathered ones now and again because I can, and because it feels like a waste of mushroom-recognition-skills if I don't. My father grew to accept these strange fungi that would turn up in stews or scrambled eggs, just as he happily went along with the mushroom strings. These were garlands of sliced fungi threaded on cotton that that my mother hung across the windows to dry on one particular holiday. As this was a hotel holiday rather than a cottage one, I dread to think what the chambermaids must have thought. Presumably this was a skill Mother had learnt from Kamila many years previously, and it felt perfectly reasonable for her to do it. The dried mushrooms were packed away in paper bags and taken home to be added to stews. They always had a slightly weird flavour. I wasn't convinced, but found myself doing exactly the same thing some years later. I eventually threw the home-dried mushrooms out. They tasted revolting and became reconstituted slime when I cooked them.

Autumn may have been the time for mushrooms and jam-making, but winter was for skiing and tobogganing. Heavy snowfalls were guaranteed in Bratislava, so cars, buses and trams had snow chains fitted as a matter of course. To reach the nearby hills for winter sports, the family would take one of the trams which throughout the winter had a trailer attached for the specific purpose of carrying the passengers' skis and toboggans.

Máňa took responsibility for teaching the younger children the basics of skiing. She started with Jirka and Pavel, while Jana and Kamila stuck to tobogganing. By the time Jana was considered old enough to ski, Jirka was at school in Prague, so Pavel had the job of looking after his baby sister, much to his disgust – Jana's words. I don't know what Pavel thought. The two of them enjoyed the downhill skiing, despite having to trudge back up the slopes as there were no ski-lifts. As an alternative, there was cross-country skiing, which I'm sure suited Kamila fine as she would meet the children at a café at the end the course. Jana enjoyed the all this skiing but wasn't particularly skilled, tending to use the poor skier's method of stopping by falling over, so most winters were marred by minor ankle injuries.

She was not so keen on skating, but still went regularly to the skating rink behind the boys' school which was open to the public in the winter. The blades for skating on would be screwed into boots, so were removable for convenience. Jana fell over often, but sometimes one of the older boys would help and give her a ride by pulling her along. I've inherited her rubbish skating skills – a few sessions in my teens at Streatham ice rink showed me I would never be any good, so I refrained from pursuing the activity and no doubt have avoided plenty of injuries as a result. My skating 'skills' could have been predicted by anyone watching me attempt to roller-skate. As for skiing, the very idea fills me with horror. Why would anyone want to slide down snow covered slopes at high speed? Feels like madness, however exhilarating it might be. My mother might have been sporty as a child, but I was emphatically not.

8

THE RUNAWAY TORTOISE AND OTHER
ANIMALS

Leo and Rézi (Terezie) Freund were Jana's favourite uncle and aunt. Rézi was Kamila's younger sister by three years. Her husband Leo worked for Českomoravská Kolben-Daněk, the same company as Gustav, but at their head office in Prague. Uncle Leo was a favourite because of his unfailing ability to make Jana laugh. He was an imposing figure and very tall for a central European, which meant that when he lifted Jana up and sat her on his shoulders she was at ceiling height. With his stature and features, Leo didn't look at all Jewish. Rézi, on the other hand, did. One day when travelling on a crowded tram, with Leo standing and Rézi sitting nearby, a colleague of Leo's said: 'What a pretty little Jewess.' Leo replied, much to his colleague's embarrassment: 'That's my wife.' The 'pretty Jewess' Aunt Rézi was a very good cook, but according to Kamila she was far too conscious of hygiene and found it difficult to accept that certain foodstuffs, like flour, could not be washed before use.

Leo and Rézi owned a villa in the suburbs of Prague, so the family often stayed with them when visiting the city. Being childless, Rézi was the aunt most likely to be able to visit Kamila and help out when necessary. Their younger sister Milada, also had no children, but as she was unmarried she was generally working so could not visit so often.

Leo and Rézi weren't the only relations in Prague. In the summer of 1936, Gustav had to visit ČKD head office in the city and took six year old Jana along for the trip. Rézi was unable to look after her for some reason on this occasion, so Gustav and Jana stayed instead with Kamila's elder brother, Uncle Viktor, and his wife Aunt Miluška instead. This couple had a son, Miloš, and Jana's outstanding memory of this particular trip was her cousin Miloš's naughty behaviour. A typical example was his putting salt in the sugar basin for a laugh. This sort of behaviour explains the close bond that developed between Miloš and Jana's eldest brother, Jirka. Both boys excelled in playing pranks on family members. At home, nobody was safe from Jirka's attention. His elder sister, Máňa, was always very smartly turned out with immaculate make- up, perfect coiffure, silk stockings and the latest fashions. On one occasion, Jirka managed to 'accidentally' snag Máňa's stockings just before she went out so that she had to change them in a hurry. Another time, in 1934 or 35, when Máňa had brought home a boyfriend, Jirka organised an 'entertainment' for the couple. This consisted of action songs, concluding with a very vulgar and scatological one which the children sang while sitting on chamber pots. Máňa and her boyfriend were greatly embarrassed, exactly as Jirka had intended.

In 1938, the last time the family were able to visit Leo and Rézi in Prague, Kamila's brother Karel, his wife Elizabeth and their then three year old daughter Marian were also present. Eight year old Jana was supposed to play with Marian, but the little girl didn't speak any Czech – her mother was German – and Jana only had a few words of German, so this wasn't very successful. Marian, at just three years old, was also an opinionated little girl. When she and her parents were due to leave, Leo went out to get his car to take give them a lift home. As soon as Marian understood what was happening, she got cross and kept repeating, 'Ich will mit Trolleybus fahren!' (I want to go by trolleybus!) as she was fed up with going everywhere by car. I've met Marian, and can't imagine her as a tiny tot stamping her feet and insisting on having her way, but perhaps she was frustrated and tired after an afternoon of non-communication with her older cousin.

Leo bred canaries as a hobby. He thought Jana might like one as a present, so one time when Gustav was visiting, he gave him one to take back to Bratislava. The bird was well-received, but appeared lonely, so the family decided to get it a mate. One thing led to another, and Gustav ended up as a canary breeder himself. The family always kept the original pair, Petřík (Peterkin) and Věrka (Little Vera), along with a pair of the latest generation, but gave any others away. In the summer, the canaries' cage was placed on the back balcony where the young birds, being natural mimics, learnt to chirp like sparrows.

In the course of my researches, I came across a short film clip of the composer Franz Lehár in Vienna in the 1930s playing the piano with his pet canary sitting on his shoulder. Maybe canaries in the interbellum Austro-Hungarian Empire were as ubiquitous as budgies during my own childhood in England, where many of my friends had one. I asked my mother about this, and yes, absolutely right.

Keeping caged birds seems reasonable enough, but I wouldn't have thought people living in a third floor apartment who needed to go by public transport to reach their garden would even consider keeping a tortoise as a pet. Jana and her brothers still had one, which they kept it in a sort of a hutch on one of the apartment's balconies. It didn't always live there. Perhaps due to an awareness of the dull life it must be living, the children took it with them when they went to visit some friends. The tortoise was let loose in the garden for a wander around, but it made a break for it and 'ran' away. The distraught children thought it was lost for good, but it re-appeared the following spring having safely hibernated through the winter and was taken back to its high rise home on the balcony.

The tortoise and the canaries are reliably documented, but I'm still having problems sorting out the dogs. I know one of Máňa's boyfriends once gave her a

Chihuahua puppy. However endearing Máňa may have found the pet, it didn't live with them for long. Gustav didn't like dogs and as the puppy insisted on climbing on his bed, it had to go. Despite Pavel's clear memories of a German Shepherd dog in the apartment block, Jana still pretty much denies its existence, though she does recall a large dog that belonged to the people who had the garden next to theirs in Nightingale Valley. This was a vicious beast, so it can't have been the one Pavel told me about. It was always kept chained up next to its kennel as there were no fences between the gardens and it wouldn't have been safe to allow it to wander freely. There's another possible contender in Jana's mind for the mysterious German Shepherd. A German/Hungarian friend of Kamila's called Mrs Török owned a large dog, and the children would have known this animal from their occasional visits to the country. She lived in a village with the rather lovely name of Harmonia on the outskirts of Modra, a village which will feature later in this story. The children certainly played with Mrs Török's dog, but this particular animal wouldn't have visited the apartment in Bratislava.

Mrs Török used to take in child boarders during the summer holidays and teach them German. Pavel and Jana spent a week with her one year, and presumably liked it well enough because when life for Jews became precarious later on, Kamila asked the Catholic Mrs Török if she could take the children in permanently. She unfortunately felt she had to refuse. Jana assumes this is because she considered the risks too great.

The tortoise and the canaries would be the last pets for many years. Circumstances wouldn't allow for any more animals until decades later when my brother and I must have badgered our mother for some sort of an animal. I'm pretty sure our first pet, when I was very small, was a goldfish called Algernon – 'Algae' for short. I didn't get the joke until years later.

9

ŠTEFÁNIKOVÁ ŠKOLA

Gustav and Kamila were what would now be called assimilated Jews. They were not at all religious, were not practising Jews, but they both came from Jewish families so the children instinctively knew that this was their heritage, even if they had no active knowledge of what that might mean. Gustav was more than non-practising; he was an active atheist and against religion of any kind. He took the unusual step for those days of withdrawing his children from all religious education at school. As a result, Jana grew up in complete ignorance of the religious practices of others, and most likely prejudiced, due to her father's opinions, against their observance. This didn't stop the family celebrating Christmas along with their friends, however. They put up a tree and enjoyed the traditional festive foods the same as everyone else. The tree was decorated on Christmas Eve with baubles, nuts, tangerines and chocolate wrapped in silver foil, lametta and tinsel, real candles, and a silver star of Bethlehem on top. It stayed up until Twelfth Night. The festival of St Nicholas was celebrated on the sixth of December by hanging up stockings the night before and finding them mysteriously filled with chocolates, fruit and nuts the following morning.

On Christmas Eve the family always ate carp, usually with potato salad. Christmas Day would start with *vánočka* for breakfast. This is a sweetish plaited loaf, which tastes somewhere between a much lighter version of Stollen and a less sweet version of panettone. I still make *vánočka* to eat for breakfast throughout the Christmas period, and as my son has now learnt to make it, the tradition looks set to continue.

Dinner on Christmas Day was eaten in the middle of the day, and started with a clear soup. The main course was a traditional roast: either goose served with knedliky and stewed cabbage with onions, or turkey served with potatoes and red cabbage with apples and onions. Neither roast bird was served with any sort of stuffing. Dessert was a gateau. In the afternoon there was the usual tea meal, but because of the season this included the special biscuits I remember scoffing down in my own childhood. I also made these once I had children of my own, and we all enjoyed the intensely flavoured chocolate biscuits, crumbling vanilla flavoured biscuits and almond crescents. My personal favourite was always, *kočiči oči* (cat's eyes) – lemon flavoured biscuits sandwiched together with redcurrant jelly. Recipes for *vánočka* and *kočiči oči* can be found at the end of the book

When she was five years old, Jana attended a nursery school run by Catholic nuns. At Christmas, she naturally took part in the Nativity play. Even Gustav wouldn't have withdrawn her from this. Jana was given the role of an angel, and in later years she wondered if the nuns had even known she was Jewish. As neither she nor Kamila had characteristic Jewish features, possibly they hadn't realised.

One of Gustav's friends, Mr Blau, thought this lack of Jewish up-bringing and practice was very wrong. In his opinion, the children were being brought up as little heathens. To counterbalance this unfortunate situation, he invited Jana to his family's Passover celebrations. Jana was happy to go as she knew Mr Blau had a daughter who was only slightly older than herself, so she looked forward to an enjoyable evening with a potential new friend. What she did not realise was that the youngest of the gathering would have an important solo role to play. Mr Blau's daughter had no doubt decided she wanted a rest from being the youngest, having dutifully performed the role for the last few years, so had asked her father to invite Jana. Perhaps she stressed that Jana was missing out on an important festival and it was her father's duty to as head of a good Jewish family to help out.

Jana was duly invited, and found herself having to ask a series of key questions about the significance and events of Passover, all in Hebrew, so that the head of the family could give the answers – also in Hebrew. Luckily for her, Mr Blau had written out the questions phonetically and provided translations. Jana was still lost, not knowing what any of it was about. The evening felt as if it were going on interminably. About the only thing that has stuck in her mind was the first question: *Ma nishtane ha-laila ha-zeh*? (What is special about this night?) She wouldn't have understood the answer as it was spoken in Hebrew, so the significance was lost on her. The meal itself contained special and important foods, but she has no recollection of these. When I prompted her, asking about the *afikoman* – which I'd learnt about from a Jewish friend – it jogged her memory, and she was able to tell me about the adults hiding something and the children having to find it and being rewarded, but she wasn't sure of any of the details. This happened a very long time ago, and it was just one evening in her childhood. The next day, she probably thought, 'I wonder what was all that about?' and dismissed it as just one of those things.

Gustav thoroughly approved of his children being brought up as 'heathens', so there was never any question about schooling – they'd attend the normal state primary school; not the Jewish alternative. Jana began her formal education in September 1936, just after her sixth birthday. The school – *Štefániková Škola* – was named after a very famous figure of the time, Milan Rastislav Štefánik. I was ashamed to say I'd never heard of him, so looked him up. The son of a Lutheran pastor, Štefánik studied construction engineering and then astronomy, physics, optics, mathematics and philosophy at Charles University in Prague. As an astronomer, he climbed Mont Blanc to observe the moon and Mars, and travelled the world making contacts with scientists, astronomers and artists everywhere, even

62

going as far afield as the Galapagos Islands. He always had a passion for politics, and hoped that the defeat of Austria-Hungary and Imperial Germany would mean the Slovaks and Czechs would gain independence. To this end, he joined the French army and trained as an aviator, flying some thirty missions. He became increasingly involved in politics in France in 1915, becaming a General in the French army and also serving as the Czech Minister of War. His travels as a diplomat took him to both Russia and the USA. When the war ended, his skills as a diplomat were in great demand. He died in 1919 when the plane he was flying in to return home to see his family in crashed, either due to the weather, or possibly shot down for political reasons. It's hardly surprising that this astonishing man became a hero – there are identical statues of him in Prague, Bratislava and Paulhan, France – and of course he was bound to have schools and other buildings named after him.

This particular *Štefániková Škola* was a modern school with spacious airy classrooms and large windows. The teacher's desk stood on a dais in front of the main blackboard. In the classrooms for the younger children, the whole of the side of one wall was taken over by a chalkboard. The children didn't have formal desks as such, but sat in twos at tables with drawers. It sounds very similar to my own primary school, except we didn't raise our teachers on a dais. None of Jana's teachers wore anything special to mark them out as teaching staff – no caps and gowns, or anything formal of that kind, either at this primary school or any of the schools she attended subsequently.

Her favourite teacher was Mrs Jelínková, who taught the alphabet by drawing pictures. The letter H was a doll lying on bed; while T had leaves to look like a tree. Jana loved everything to do with this school and lapped up the education. Most of her socialising time up to this point had been with boys, apart from the previous year at the nursery school. The all-girls environment both there and at this primary school felt very strange at first, but she soon made friends. This ease at making friends wherever she went would stand her in good stead in the years to come. I think I would have hated being in an all girls' primary school. I went to a co-educational primary, so was able to mix with my brother's friends when I tired of girly games. The boys tolerated me remarkably well for short periods. Moving to a single sex secondary school when I was eleven was horrible for me, but at that time there wasn't a choice as co-educational secondary schools were rarities.

Jirka and Pavel attended the parallel boys' primary school, but the two schools never combined for any activities. Their timetable was much the same. All the children had to be early risers, as the school day started at eight in the morning. For the first term, from September to Christmas, Jana's day was already finished by ten o'clock, but this would not have been a problem for most families because as so long as a child had two parents, the mother would not be going out to work. Married women with children simply didn't.

The emphasis during this intensive two hour introduction to school lessons was on literacy. The day was short enough that concentration didn't flag, and as the children had already reached the grand old age of six years old by the time they started school, learning to read was quick and efficient. By Christmas, all the children had a good grasp of basic literacy and could tackle other subjects easily. After Christmas, the school day increased to three hours, and later on to four. By the time the children were ten years old, the school day was a full five hours.

Much documentary evidence from Jana's past has inevitably been lost, but amazingly, her school reports have pretty much all survived. The report for 1936/37 gives her name as 'Janka Anna Gráfová'. The spelling varies slightly in different reports. Sometimes her middle name is given as 'Hana', but the first name is always given in the Slovak form of 'Janka' rather than the Czech 'Jana'. The description of the country changes – in this first report it's given as Československá Republika' but in later reports political changes take their toll. The school's name is given along

64

with her date and place of birth, and the date on which she started school. These documents are mostly tick-box style reports, with grades given for each subject from 1 for the best results down to 5 for the worst. In this first report Jana managed a 1 for basic level reading, 2 for writing and speaking, 1 for elementary science, 1 for basic arithmetic, 1 for singing, and 1 for PE, which shows she had made an excellent start, so it's not surprising she was enjoying herself so much. The following year, the marks were very similar – 1 for reading, 2 for writing and speaking, 1 for elementary science in the first term, though this dropped to 2 by the end of the year, 2 for arithmetic, 2 for singing, 1 for PE. Unfortunately it's beyond me to decipher the beautiful cursive script at the end of the report which presumably gives general comments, but I would assume they were very encouraging given the overall marks.

There was no school uniform as such, but all the girls wore a navy apron to protect their clothes. This was kept at school, and would have been similar to the overalls the children in the infants' classes attached to my secondary school used to wear. At my own state primary school I had to suffer the full school uniform of scratchy green gymslip, green beret with a yellow tassel, and gingham summer dresses. I always liked the blazer, which was probably the most impractical item, but wasn't keen on the rest, especially not the socks that always fell down despite having home-sewn elastic garters to keep them up. I think the rubber in old-style elastic must have perished quickly. My own clothes plus an apron would have been preferable.

Jana didn't have any particular favourite clothes at this time. She usually wore dresses or skirts, with jumpers or blouses. These would be cotton in the summer and woollen in winter. On holidays she might occasionally wear a navy tracksuit passed on from her brothers. There was just one very daring 'modern' garment – cotton striped dungarees. I've seen a photo, and this is precisely the sort of thing I used to make for my own daughters. Apart from ordinary winter coats, there was also a *Hubertus*, a dark green hooded coat made from *Loden*, which was thick felted water resistant wool. This garment originated as Austrian peasant garb and was similar to a duffel coat, though with ordinary buttons rather than toggles. I've looked it up – these coats still exist, but nowadays, they appear to have become expensive fashion items.

Jana wore stockings in winter, held up by suspenders attached to a bodice, which was usually beige, but white for special occasions. As presumably this wouldn't have been visible under whatever else she was wearing, I have no idea why the colour changed, though I suppose 'special' underwear for best is the sort of thing we all do, with no real logic behind it. Once the outdoor temperatures reached 16C, the stockings were discarded and replaced by knee length socks. These were never white, as that was the official sock colour of the Hitler Youth movement. In high summer, the long socks were replaced by short ones. Footwear was shoes or sandals in the summer, and lace-up boots in winter. All shoes were brown, apart from one special pair of red bar shoes. Once at school, although there was no specific uniform, the clothing would be more formal. The stripy dungarees, for example, would never have been worn. Jana was generally dressed in a navy pleated skirt and a white shirt. The shirt was definitely a shirt and not a blouse, as it would be a hand-me-down previously worn by Pavel. Some clothes were ready-made, but some were made by Kamila, who along with various aunts would hand knit jumpers and cardigans. The thickest jumpers were reserved for skating or tobogganing, along with woollen leggings

Jana's best friend at *Štefániková Škola* was a Slovak girl called Zuzka Jukerová who was an only child. This friendship gave Jana much needed respite from her brothers. She loved going round to Zuzka's house to play as it was always so quiet, with no boys fighting and arguing and no sides to take. Although Kamila didn't say anything, Jana had the impression that her mother didn't approve of Zuzka's family. This little girl was often left alone with the maid in the afternoon while her mother went off to play bridge, and

Kamila considered that the maid spoiled the child rotten by doing everything for her – even tying her shoe laces, which any self-respecting six year old should have been able to do for herself.

Another primary school friend was a Czech girl called Vera Kluková, whose father was a policeman. This idea frightened Jana for some reason. I wonder if she'd seen the sort of old-fashioned story book in which the policeman is always the terrifying authority figure who metes out punishments to naughty little children. That could have accounted for the fear. I was nervous of a friend's policeman father myself at a similar age, possibly for the same reasons.

Jana was also friends with a Slovak girl called Karla Dolinárová around this time. Karla came from a one-parent family and Kamila made Jana promise never to talk to Karla about her father. Jana couldn't understand why this was, or how, indeed, there could be a family without a father, especially one who couldn't be mentioned. She longed to know what had happened to cause this situation, but didn't dare ask. Karla was often invited to tea – more often than Zuzka, although Zuzka was Jana's preferred friend. Karla was a skinny child and always hungry, so Kamila must have wanted to make sure she had a good meal now and again. When the school's Parent Teacher Association made their regular collections of second hand clothes, Kamila, as a committee member, always made sure some were reserved for Karla. Jana found out later that Karla's father was in prison – hence his absence and the taboo on mentioning his existence. There must have been children in similar situations amongst my own friends, but I can't honestly remember any, so I suspect that sort of thing was still taboo.

In Jana's second year, the school put on a show for all the parents in celebration of the anniversary of the founding of Czechoslovakia. Jana's class performed a dance where all the girls were dressed in red, white and blue; the colours of the national flag. She was also chosen to recite a poem – her first solo performance – and must have learnt it extremely well, as she was able to tell me the words with no difficulty.

Nad školou nám prápor vlaje,
Vietor si s ním pekne hraje.
To sa iste niečo deje,
Červená sa s bielou smeje
A modrá im napomáha
Sviatok má vlást naša drahá.

A flag is waving above the school,
The wind is playing with it,
Something must be happening,
Red and white are smiling
Blue is helping
Our dear country is celebrating

I have no doubt this is an accurate memory, but I have no idea how my mother has managed to retain the words for all these years. I'm sure I must have been in school plays aged seven, but I'd be hard pressed to relate anything much about them. Just one stands out at this distance. I was in the second year juniors at Wickham Common Primary school, aged nine or ten, when I had my first solo speaking role. My class was performing *Babar the Elephant* and I played a little old lady. Despite having read them over and over again, and tried my hardest to memorise them, I had no idea in either rehearsals or performance as to what my lines were supposed to be and had to guess them with some helpful prompts from the wings by the teacher, Mr Cousins. Years later, at secondary school, I had an even more pathetic acting experience. We were performing Bertold Brecht's *Galileo* – a ridiculous play for an all girls school to produce, as it only has one female role, but never mind. I played a 'very old cardinal'. I had one speech. Could I recite it? Of course not – I had to improvise yet again, to my shame. The fact that my mother can still knows all the words from a poem recited at age seven gives me confidence that many more of her other memories are more accurate than I initially thought.

Jana wasn't the only one of the children to shine that year. Her eldest brother Jirka was chosen to appear on the radio to broadcast best wishes and thanks on behalf of all Slovak primary schools on the occasion of President Masaryk's birthday. The family found it highly amusing that a Czech Jew should be chosen for this honour – and we're up against that humour problem again, and my own non-comprehension. Surely a child living in Slovakia and attending a Slovak school counts as Slovak? I'm clearly missing some nuances here. I also don't know fully understand why it should have been such an issue, at that point, that he was from a Jewish background. He must have been a bright child and well spoken and that is why he was chosen – but the rise of Hitler at that time presumably was already affecting ethnic and religious identity in ways I cannot now imagine. A certain amount of anti-Semitism had no doubt always been there, but now it must have been a worrying issue, even though no one could yet imagine how bad things were to become.

When not reciting patriotic poetry, Jana was gaining a thorough grounding in the basics of reading, writing, arithmetic, singing and PE. Subjects like history, geography and science would be introduced later. The first modern foreign language – German – was not started until the children were eight years old. There should have been religious instruction as well, but of course Gustav had withdrawn his children from any such unwelcome indoctrination and brainwashing.

Jana first major illness happened when she contracted scarlet fever at age six or seven. She'd already gone through all the other common childhood ailments, thanks to her brothers bringing them home from school, but this was different, and far more serious. Nowadays scarlet fever is rarely an issue as it is easily treated by penicillin and similar antibiotics, but I've checked the dates, and penicillin had only been

69

discovered eight years previously, so was still many years off being a standard treatment. As a result, scarlet fever was a nasty disease and would normally have meant incarceration in an isolation hospital, but Kamila persuaded the doctor to let her care for Jana at home. The doctor agreed, provided the other children were sent away. Pavel and Jirka went to stay with friends of the family – possibly a former maid of Kamila's from way back, a Mrs Bastiánová, who had married a farmer and now lived in the country. Kamila had always bought the Christmas turkey from these people, which is how they had kept in touch. Máňa went to stay with her own friends, on the other staircase in the same block of flats, a family called Novák who re-appear much later in this story.

The period of isolation lasted a full two months. Towards the end of this time, Kamila would wrap Jana up well and sit her by an open window – a bit like hardening off a tender plant. Kamila believed that the full cure was mostly down to the copious supply of citrus fruits. She may well have been right. All that vitamin C must have helped. One activity Jana particularly enjoyed during her convalescence was playing with pieces of marzipan which she moulded into pretend fruits and vegetables and then ate.

In about 1937 or 38, the government decided all children should attend their nearest school. Unfortunately the family was living outside the official catchment area for *Štefánikova Škola*. Gustav and Kamila objected to the change of school, and the staff of the girl's department of *Štefánikova Škola* wanted Jana to stay there – possibly because she was one of their brightest pupils – so she did. The boy's school however, was adamant that Pavel couldn't stay, so he had to go to a more local school called *Hodžova Škola*. He was very unhappy there as his teacher was a rabid anti-Semite, and always referred to Pavel not by his name but as 'that Jew'. Years later, when Pavel had emigrated to the United States, Uncle Karel tried to get him to accept his Jewishness, but found it difficult. He only understood this reluctance when Jana told him about Pavel's primary school experiences.

Both Kamila and Gustav were voracious readers. Jana had always been allowed to choose her own reading matter as it was her father's belief that she wouldn't be inclined to read anything beyond her understanding, and if she did understand it, that proved she was ready to read it. The mother of one of Jana's school friends was horrified when told what the ten year old Jana was reading, but this is hardly surprising. Kamila was in the habit of buying all the latest novels, so Jana might have been reading a piece of contemporary fiction with very adult themes.

Many of the children's books she read were in translation. All the classics were available – many of which I also read at a similar age. Among the books Jana enjoyed were Kipling's *Just So Stories* and *The Jungle Book*, Arthur Ransome's *Swallows and Amazons*, the *Just William* stories, many Russian romances, Jules Verne, D'Annunzio's stories, Erich Kästner's *Emil and the Detectives* and his other stories, Karel Čapek's short stories and Czech and Slovak folk tales, as well as other children's tales which were lying around at home anyway because her brothers were reading them. Fairy tales as such didn't interest her as she wanted stories with real people. That's what she's always said. 'Real people'. No giants and ogres and fairies and dragons as they're not real apparently. Okay, so what about the *Just So Stories*? What about *The Jungle Book*? They're full of talking animals, but they're so incredibly real, I've a feeling she hasn't noticed the discrepancy in her argument. Quite apart from the talking animals, what about Jules Verne? He wrote science fiction, which is futuristic so hardly 'real' in her terms – except, of course, that the best animal stories, the best fantasy, and the best sci-fi are all as real as any literary fiction, and fairy stories are equally real as they're metaphors for real life situations – cautionary tales about families with step-parents, about dangers in the forest, about the whims of the ruling classes, about rescue when all hope seems lost.

71

My own reading matter as a child coincided in some areas, but veered off sharply in others. Kipling – yes, couldn't get enough of him. Still love his stories, including the children's ones. Folk tales, myths and legends, also yes. As regards fairy tales, very much so, but they had to be the ones collected by the Brothers Grimm, not those weedy things by Hans Christian Andersen with what I saw as feeble characters and sentimentality. I far preferred the powerful archetypes that could be found in the Grimm Brother's dramatic tales, with their proper heroes and real monsters. It's interesting; the more I find out these details about my mother's early life, the more I realise how much we differed. She had brothers to play with, and presumably their friends, yet preferred to play with the girls at school. I'm getting the impression she was much more gregarious than I was when young; keen to get into the whole area of traditional girls' play where I always far preferred playing with the boys next door and my brother's school friends. When I played with girls, it would be with a select few who shared interests like drawing, or making up stories – I never liked to play in a group. Perhaps after all I'm more like my uncle Pavel than my mother; more of a loner and an introvert. As a result, this getting into my mother's young head is proving extraordinarily difficult. I knew plenty of girls like her at school; chatty friendly girls who enjoyed all the traditional roles that they played in their games, but I was never one of them.

She'll probably read this and say she was nothing like my impression of her at all, but I'm starting to understand the roots of some of the blank incomprehension we both feel nowadays when talking about our preferences in literature or music. This, however, was the end of a normal girlhood for my mother. Pavel's experience of vicious anti-Semitism at his own school had given a hint of what was to come. It wouldn't be long before the whole family would start to experience the horrors of how far this sort of thing could go when it became officially sanctioned, so this is point where my own childhood experiences and those of my mother start to veer away from each other dramatically and become unimaginably different; where the search for my 'hidden mother' really begins.

PART TWO

10

A NEW SCHOOL

Máňa hasn't appeared much in this account so far as she was so much older than Jana, and a sixteen year age difference is a lifetime when you are very young. Jana was only eight or nine years old when Máňa disappeared out of her life. She wouldn't reappear until after the war. One of Jana's clearest early memories is of Máňa's wedding in 1938 to the opera singer Otto (Otakar) Kraus. Many of the family's relations in Prague, including uncles and aunts who were rarely seen otherwise, came across to Bratislava for the wedding. The ceremony took place in a register office, with just the parents and witnesses present, not the rest of the family. This was followed by a lunch at the flat for the family, but the bridegroom couldn't stay for his own wedding lunch. He had to rush off to a rehearsal straight after the ceremony as he was appearing in a production at the National Theatre that evening, and the mere fact of getting married wouldn't be enough to break the old 'the show must go on' adage. Rehearsal over, he returned for the rest of the reception which was being held at a hotel by a lake on the outskirts of town at a place called Železná Studánka. The celebrations went on very late, and Jana was put to bed in one of the hotel rooms that an uncle had booked. Mr Novák, the father of the friend Máňa had stayed with when Jana had scarlet fever, was the only person Jana saw get really drunk – but as she had been put to bed early, who knows how sozzled the rest of them became later on.

Opera singers are rarely early risers, and Otto was no exception. He always liked to have a lie-in after performances. Jana's eldest brother Jirka knew this, so every once in a while he rang Otto's number early in the morning just for the hell of it. On one occasion he rang to say Otto's favourite cousin was arriving in Bratislava by a very early train. Otto rose in a panic, dressed quickly and hurried to the station, but of course no cousin appeared. Otto wasn't Jirka's only victim. On another occasion, Jirka sent what Jana thought looked like a blackmailing or threatening note to the family GP. One can only hope the poor doctor saw the joke.

In 1937, while Jana was still at primary school, Jirka made the fateful decision to pursue his secondary education in Prague rather than Bratislava. He reasoned that a Czech Gymnasium – a grammar school equivalent – would give him a better education in a more widely spoken language than the equivalent school at home. This was no doubt true, but Pavel thinks this wasn't the only reason for Jirka's decision. The two brothers were always fighting, and Pavel thinks Gustav and Kamila might have thought they would both benefit by being separated for a while. Jana now thinks it was probably a combination of both reasons. It wasn't just the fighting. Jirka was obviously very gifted and their parents might have felt Pavel would do better without always feeling he had to compete academically. Jirka was only eleven at the time, so this was a huge step. I can imagine Gustav and Kamila reluctantly agreeing, in the knowledge that he would, undoubtedly receive a better and more useful education in Prague, but hating the thought of their talented livewire son going away before he had even reached his teens. I'm sure there was much discussion, but in the end Jirka, who was very keen for this to happen prevailed and the decision was made. He packed his bags and went to live with Kamila's sister Aunt Rézi and her husband Uncle Leo in Prague.

For the first year, all was fine. Jirka settled into his new school and came home for the school holidays, but in 1938, the political disruption and economic uncertainty in

Europe started coming to a head. There had been problems and a certain amount of unrest since the Locarno Treaties of 1925, but now, due to the Munich Agreement of September 1938, the various regions ceased to exist in their current states. First of all Sudetenland was occupied by Nazi Germany; then the remainder of the country was remained Czecho-Slovakia. At first Slovakia had a certain amount of autonomy, but Southern and Eastern Slovakia were reclaimed by Hungary at the First Vienna Award of November 1938. By this time Hitler was preparing to invade the Czech regions of Bohemia and Moravia, and also had further plans for Slovakia. The Germans were told that the remaining Slovaks wanted to join Hungary, but this was misinformation. Jozef Tiso, who had been deposed by Czech troops as Slovak prime minister, was invited to Berlin where Hitler told him to proclaim Slovakia's independence. If he didn't agree, he would get no help from Germany, and Slovakia would be left to Poland and Hungary to carve up as they wished. Tiso did what Hitler wanted. Slovakia became an independent state, but allied to Germany. This First Slovak Republic was effectively a puppet regime of Nazi Germany, which saw it as a potential strategic base from which it could attack Poland and other regions. Needless to say, the border between the two parts of Czechoslovakia was now closed and Jirka had no way of getting across the border to see his parents.

Seeing the way things were going, Máňa and Otto arranged to emigrate while they still could. This was shortly after they had got married. Their papers were all in order, and Máňa had even managed to get permission to go to Prague to say goodbye to Jirka before she left. This made her the last member of the immediate family to see him alive. Communication became increasingly difficult, and it wasn't until years later that anyone knew what had happened to him.

Máňa and Otto weren't the only family members to decide they should get out sooner rather than later. Gustav's sister Herma – the seamstress who had made the clothes for

79

Jana's dolls – managed to leave Vienna with her son Dolfi. They emigrated to Haifa, in Israel. Herma's other son Gusti and his wife Greta also left Vienna and managed to reach Chicago while they still could. Kamila's brother Karel had also emigrated to the United States with his wife Elizabeth and daughter Marian once he saw the way things were going for academics. These family members got out in the nick of time. The process wasn't easy for any of them, particularly Máňa and Otto, whose dramatic journey I detail in a later chapter, but at least they were safe.

Another of Kamila's brothers, Viktor, and his wife Miluška, took the risk of staying put and didn't leave Prague. Miluška was a staunch Roman Catholic, the first in the family, so the family considered they would be safe from deportation. Luckily for them, they were right. I never met Miluška, but once, as a child, I did an oil painting – a copy of a Jacob Ruisdael – that my mother sent to her. I'd probably done little drawings for her before and she'd expressed an interest. She wrote back, thanking me. The letter was in an immaculate cursive script, and I couldn't read a word of it as it was in Czech, but it remained a treasured possession, a real link with the past. I still have it somewhere stored away with other childhood mementoes. Miluška never left Prague, eventually dying there in 1983 at the age of 88.

Not one of Gustav and Kamila's other brothers and sisters survived.

From 1938, all Jewish children living in the first Slovak Republic (*prvá Slovenská republika*), also known as the Slovak State (*slovenský štát*) had to attend Jewish schools whether they were practising Jews or not. There were two such schools in Bratislava, one Orthodox, and the other 'Modern', for want of a better term. Jana and Pavel inevitably went to the Modern one. As Jana knew nothing about Judaism she felt completely lost at first, just as she had at the Passover supper at Mr Blau's house, but despite this she quickly made friends. Her new best friend was a girl called Vera Schlesinger. Vera was very bright and hardworking and always aimed to gain the highest marks in class. One month when she failed to reach the top spot, she was so distraught she wept openly, to Jana's astonishment. I would have reacted very differently to Vera. Whenever I received unexpectedly low marks for homework or exams, I would assume the teacher was an idiot. I was taught by many idiots. This could well be the reason why some of my teachers decided I had an attitude problem. I remain 'awkward' with authority figures to this day.

Another best friend from this school was a girl called Hana Lipnerová – a girl with a sense of humour. When the teacher called 'Hana', both she and Jana would stand up, just for fun. I can just imagine the stifled giggles. Hana was always very nicely dressed, and Jana wanted the same clothes. The seriously academic girl, Vera, grew very jealous of this light-hearted relationship. She was the only person Jana knew at the Jewish school who after the war managed to return from a concentration camp, though minus her parents. They managed to find each other again, and stayed in touch for a while after Jana came to England, but then lost contact again and Jana hasn't heard from her since.

The state primary school had been for girls only, but the Jewish school was co-educational. This was the first time Jana had came across young boys who weren't afraid of being punished for bad behaviour. Typical pranks included writing rude words on the chalkboard and hiding books – exactly the sort of low level mischief one would expect. Nothing changes. On one memorable day, a boy hid a live grass snake in the register folder. The teacher screamed when she opened the folder and pandemonium broke out. Like many of her pupils, she had no idea the snake was harmless. Most present would have been certain it was a venomous adder.

The core curriculum at the Jewish school was identical to that of the state schools, but there were some additional subjects. Jana now had to learn Hebrew – a language she has pretty much forgotten, in much the same way I have forgotten virtually all the Ancient Greek I was taught. I just about know the alphabet, but can't read or understand any words or phrases any more as it's not a language I come across day to day. Jana also had to attend religious education lessons. There would be no option of withdrawing from such things in this school, so for the first time in her life she was exposed to the Hebrew Bible. Whatever one's views on religion, biblical writings are of huge cultural significance and a passing familiarity with them is no bad thing, if only to engage more effectively with religious art and music.

The Hebrew language lessons may not have stuck, but other new aspects of the curriculum did. It comes as no surprise that Jana enjoyed learning the Jewish dances, given her love of all things to do with music and movement. These were circle dances so didn't require a partner. Some were highly energetic, like the *horah,* which is typically danced to the music of *Hava Nagila*, on old Ukrainian folk melody. It was very easy to learn. The children formed a circle, holding hands and executed a simple step pattern while circling round. With enough dancers taking part, it could be danced in concentric circles. The music would gradually increase in pace, and the trick was not to trip over your feet. Another dance Jana enjoyed was the *Kacha Tenatzchi*. The title translates as 'Like this you will be victorious'. As with the horah, this was originally adapted from an Eastern European dance, as were most Jewish dances and melodies of the period. It could be danced to any tune with a suitable speed and rhythm, and was less frantic than the horah, though with similar footwork plus some turns.

These were often songs as well as dances. These are the words for a typical sung version of a Kacha Tenatzchi:

על ראשך אשים פרחים
בעיני אורות דולקים
שירת ליבי. בואי ואשיר לך את
כל דקה וכל שניה
יש סיבה לאהבה
תכבשי כל צער ככה תנצחי

I will put flowers on your head
in my eyes are lights [alight]
come and I will sing my heart's song
every minute every second
there's a reason for love
conquer all sorrow and like this you will be victorious

The teachers at the Jewish school were very different to the ones Jana had known at her previous school. The universities were no longer permitted to employ Jews, so all the Jewish professors had lost their jobs and many ended up teaching in primary schools, lecturing confused small children rather than highly educated young adults. These professors had varying degrees of success in this endeavour, as can be imagined. The outstanding teacher at Jana's school was a Professor Rosenblüth. He had been a professor of mathematics at the University of Bratislava, but while the change from lecturing big people to teaching small people might have been a personal disappointment to him, as far as the children were concerned this was the best thing that could have happened. His charismatic personality inspired the young pupils and made mathematics fascinating for them all. Jana loved his lessons. The grounding in maths he provided had long lasting benefits. She claims she's never yet found a maths problem beyond her thanks to his brilliant teaching. Years later she discovered he had been one of her Uncle Karel's students at Karlovy (Charles) University in Prague.

None of the other ex-university lecturers managed the same level of inspirational teaching. The language barrier was often at the heart of the problem. Jews in

Czechoslovakia at that time would be as likely to speak German or Hungarian as Slovak. The Austro-Hungarian Empire had ceased to operate as a single entity only twenty years earlier at the end of the First World War, so it was inevitable that its multi-national population wouldn't have neatly and conveniently divided itself between the individual nation states. Intellectuals in particular would have been used to feeling equally at home in any of the major universities of the former member countries, but now many of them found themselves in the position of teaching primary age children in a language they'd never thought they'd have to speak to any degree of fluency. One poor teacher at the school barely spoke a word of Slovak, but still had to teach in the language.

Despite the variable quality of the lessons and the increasingly perturbing political climate, there could still be plenty of fun for the children. In the winter the caretaker went out first thing in the morning and sprayed the school yard with water from a hose so that by break time it was frozen and the children could don skates and go outside for traditional wintertime fun. The boys inevitably took over the centre of the yard to play fast and furious games of ice hockey, while the girls skated more sedately around the edges. I'm sure nobody wore any safety gear, and there must have been accidents, but I suppose given the customary harsh winters everyone was used to slipping over on ice and hurting themselves, so nothing was thought of it.

Things were very different when I was at school. One winter's day, a girl slipped on a tiny patch of ice outside the school canteen. She reappeared with her broken arm in plaster a short while later and told us all smugly that her parents were going to sue the school, which struck me as completely absurd.

That winter Jana had another opportunity to shine in a solo performance. She was cast as the lead in a play called *Gabriela's Dream* as part of the Chanukah celebrations. Her elation at being the eponymous star of the show soon faded when she found out she would have to wear a nightie throughout, while the other children would be dressed as all manner of toys – teddy bears and rabbits and dolls. I probably felt much the same as the little old lady in *Babar the Elephant*, though I can't for the life of me remember what Babar's elephant costume looked like.

Jana's first school report for the academic year 1938/39 from the new school was in the same format as the ones from her last school, but with some notable differences. The printed name of the country at the top of the sheet (*Slovenská Krajina*) was crossed out and replaced with a stamp saying *Slovenský Štát*. Where her religion had to be given, she was now officially Jewish. Needless to say the marks were still very good – mostly 1s and 2s; the only 3s being for first term maths, and girls' handicrafts/housekeeping, though these marks both improved in subsequent terms.

In the report for the following year, 1939/40, the country name was given as *Slovenská Republika*. Her marks were again very good, the only 3 being for 'regional' studies, part of Humanities. By 1940/41, she had clearly settled well into the new way of learning, whatever the challenges of some of the teaching, because every single mark for every subject was a 1. I wonder if having a bright friend like Vera helped. I know in my own schooling, sitting next to a very clever girl in maths classes spurred me to try to work at her pace, and I pretty much succeeded. Mostly, however, I suspect it was a question of attitude. She wanted to learn, she wanted to lap up all this information – this was a trait that would follow her all the way through her schooling, even in the chaotic years that were to follow. Perhaps the rigours of academia provided a stability; an escape from the uncertainties of the outside world, where everything she knew was beginning to disintegrate.

11

A WORLD GOING MAD

Bratislava was only an hour's bus ride from Vienna where Aunt Herma lived, so the family knew what was happening in Austria from the first Nazi coup attempt in 1934 to the declaration of the Anschluss in March 1938 when Hitler announced the re-unification of Austria with Germany. The stripping of assets of all Jewish citizens was enshrined in law shortly afterwards. Jana was too young to understand exactly what was going on at the time, but she was fully aware of the political discussions that were happening at home. Her parents' friends came round most evenings to discuss the situation; analysing what had happened, what might happen, and what – if anything – they could do about it. These discussions took place when Jana was tucked up in bed, theoretically asleep in the next room, but she couldn't sleep at such times. The political talk centred on the persecution of Jews everywhere. Jana heard snippets of the conversation and felt very frightened as a result. 'Very frightened' feels like an understatement, but I don't know how else to word it without slipping into hyperbole. I have never been in an equivalent situation, so however vivid my imagination, I can't come close to understanding what it must have been like. On the one hand, it was necessary for Jana to comprehend some of the changes that were happening in her life – like the reasons why she had to go to the Jewish school – but on the other, to learn about such things in terms she wouldn't have been able to understand, aware that she shouldn't have been listening, must have been traumatising.

Kamila had heard about the *Kindertransport* in 1939, and hoped Pavel and Jana might be able to join it and be removed from the imminent danger that way. This rescue mission, also known as the Refugee Children Movement, rescued a total of 10,000 mostly Jewish children. It had been set up swiftly following the *Kristallnacht*, the 'Night of Broken Glass' on 9th-10th November 1938, when a series of vicious co-ordinated attacks against Jews had taken place throughout Nazi Germany and Austria. At least 91 died in the attacks themselves, and 30,000 were arrested and incarcerated in concentration camps. *The Times*, on 11th November 1938, wrote this report under the headline 'A Black Day for Germany': *No foreign propagandist bent upon blackening Germany before the world could outdo the tale of burnings and beatings, of blackguardly assaults on defenceless and innocent people, which disgraced that country yesterday.*

Within three weeks of these horrific events, the first group of nearly two hundred children arrived in Harwich. At first, the children were mainly from Germany and Austria, but in March 1939, additional transport was organised from Prague. Trains from Poland were also arranged, and the very last of these trains left the Netherlands in May 1940. No transport ever operated from Slovakia itself. Those children who had managed to secure places were placed in British foster homes and hostels during the nine months prior to the outbreak of the Second World War. The British government had passed an emergency bill to waive immigration rules so that unaccompanied children could be allowed into the country.

As fascism took hold, many adult Jews gave serious consideration to re-locating to England or the United States due to the obvious risk of staying where they were. When Hitler annexed Austria, this took on a new urgency and many people doubled their efforts to learn English. Those considering emigrating to England or the States would ask each other, *Sind sie Arish oder lernen sie English*? (Are you Aryan, or are you learning English?) the subtext being: are you members of a Germanic tribe (Christians) or are you learning English because you are Jewish?

It's one thing watching films about the period and learning at a comfortable and safe distance about Anne Frank and Schindler's List – quite another trying to get inside the head of a pre-teen girl, huddled in bed, hearing snippets of terrifying conversations, longing to sleep, afraid to sleep – and knowing this girl is my own mother.

As the months went by and more and more teachers were deported, the falling staffing levels meant the Modern and Orthodox schools had to amalgamate in order to remain viable. The Orthodox school's building could no longer be used, so all the children were squeezed together into the Modern school. 'Modern' is something of a misnomer in this context as the school was housed in a traditional-style old building with little daylight and gloomy corridors – very different to the state primary school Jana had attended previously. There were other difficulties. The Orthodox children had strict rules about segregation and had to be separated by gender for their education, so the Modern children had no choice but to follow suit. Keeping the sexes apart was extremely difficult in the warren of passages and corridors. The classes became seriously overcrowded as the school had been full even before the addition of the children from the Orthodox school. There weren't enough classrooms for each year group to have its own room, so different years were taught together. Too few teachers, some with no experience of teaching youngsters and poor language skills, trying to deliver a curriculum to mixed aged groups in too small classrooms must have made life impossibly difficult for all concerned. When the problems became insurmountable and the number of teachers dropped too low, the inevitable happened and the school was closed. The building was quickly requisitioned, so re-opening wasn't an option. Some parents tried to keep classes going in private houses, but even these couldn't be made to work. Jana and Pavel, like so many others, were left with no education.

By 1943, when Jana was thirteen, it became clear that the only way for her to have any sort of schooling was to be baptised. This would theoretically enable a return to the non-religious state system. There wouldn't be any access to academically rigorous grammar school style education, which would have been the preferred system given her abilities, but it would be better than nothing. The decision for the whole family to be baptised would have been particularly galling for Gustav because of his antipathy to religion of any kind, but he had to be pragmatic. There was more at stake here than simply his children's schooling. This was about survival.

Pastor Jurkovič, the Lutheran priest who baptised them, knew he wasn't making converts, but he went ahead anyway, like many other philanthropic clerics at the time, out of a sense of common humanity and the knowledge that this was the right thing to do. He was saving people – not in the Christian sense, but in a very practical and realistic way, so he baptised as many as he could. This had to be done carefully. It wouldn't do to baptise all the family members at the same time as that would draw too much attention and could be dangerous. Gustav and Kamila were baptised first, so that when the priest came to do the children later on he could legitimately write on their baptismal certificates that their parents were Lutheran. The arrangements were made, and the baptisms carried out, but when it came to Gustav's turn he stumbled over the words of the Creed having failed to memorise them properly, and had to be prompted. His witness, Mr Rybák – the father of the children's friend Vláďa from the apartments over the showroom – was Christian, but very Low Church, so refused to kneel where he was supposed to during the ritual. I suppose Gustav knew he had to go through with this, but was determined to show his dislike of the whole process in the only way he could without derailing everything.

Máňa had also made sure she was baptised before she left Slovakia. She later claimed she'd asked a prostitute she'd met on the street to act as a witness, but Jana has her doubts, thinking it was more likely an acquaintance. I like Máňa's story so am including it in this account anyway. It's perfectly plausible that Máňa met this woman randomly, asked her to be a witness, and didn't find out what she did for a living until afterwards.

As far as Jana and Pavel were concerned, being baptised made no difference to them in faith terms as neither had become practising Jews despite the best efforts of the Jewish school, but at least it meant they could now resume their education. That was the theory. In the event, Jana and Pavel attended the state secondary school for such a short time that Jana can't tell me anything about it, but at least having been baptised they could stop wearing the hated yellow star during this brief period. All Jews had been forced to wear the Star of David badge in order to identify themselves as being Jewish. The rules insisted that it be visible at all times regardless of the clothing being worn, so in winter Jana had been wearing it on her outer coat, but in summer it would be on her cardigan. The children soon found ways of carrying their school bags to cover the star up. This sort of subterfuge became second nature. They learnt, if not exactly to lie, at least to hide the truth of their origins.

Even after she had been baptised, Jana tried to avoid answering questions about her previous school. She thinks this privateness and need for secrecy stayed with her for a very long time. Perhaps it's still there, and this is one of the reasons she didn't tell me and my brother as much as she thinks she did about her background when we were little. The instinct to hide would have been strong, despite her conscious view that it's vitally important for people to know what went on so that such things can be prevented in the future. If histories are not known, people plunge headlong into making the same mistakes again and again – so the testimony of witnesses must be recorded. The problem is that however much you know and approve the premise, breaking through the barrier of imposed silence is still very difficult in later years.

For Kamila, who was a most truthful and upright person, teaching her children to be the opposite must have hurt deeply. She looked pure Aryan due to her light brown hair and blue eyes, so was often mistaken for a German. People on the streets collecting aid money for German soldiers would assume she was one of them and approach her to ask for a donation. She'd delight in showing them her yellow star, so while she was not exactly proud of wearing the wretched thing, at least it enabled her to keep a sense of identity in a world going mad.

12

DOWNSIZING

I need to backtrack a little here. As well as schooling becoming increasingly problematic, there was also the whole issue of where to live. The family was never going to be allowed to stay in their spacious and well-equipped apartment overlooking the National Theatre, not with the way things were going.

In March 1939, following the separation of Slovakia from the Protectorate of Bohemia and Moravia, Gustav was forced out of his job with ČKD and pensioned off. His pension was paid in Prague, so it was impossible for him to receive it as he was living in Bratislava. There was no way round this, so he didn't get a penny. As he was no longer an employee, he was told he would have to vacate the apartment above the showroom by the end of the year. The family had no income at this point, so were surviving by selling off the greater part of Gustav's prized collection of artworks and ornaments. Some of the paintings were sold outright, other pawned to raise cash, but as Gustav would never return to redeem them, this came ultimately to the same thing. The piano was to be given to some friends to look after, but the people in question later denied this so it's impossible now to find out what happened to the instrument.

I was given a violin in my teens that had 'been in the family' and allegedly belonged to a distant relative who'd been a great violinist. I received this wondrous instrument when I was deemed sufficiently proficient to be worthy of handling it. The violin turned out to be a lemon – and the bow was a banana. Violinists will know what I mean. That is to say, bow and violin looked decent enough if you didn't know much about fine instruments, but clearly had never belonged to a concert violinist. The violin was a badly cracked Stainer model with a wildly exaggerated shape – a cheap nineteenth century German model with pretty enough wood on the back, but a thin and weedy tone. The unnamed, nickel-mounted bow had a bend in it that went the wrong way. I persevered with this equipment for years, assuming it was my technique that was stopping me getting the brilliant sound the previous owner must have managed. It was only when we had the violin valued for insurance purposes that the truth emerged. The people who had looked after the violin during the war had almost certainly sold the original, made a load of money on the deal, and bought this cheap one as a substitute in case they were ever asked to return the instrument. I eventually traded it in for a cheapish French violin that was exactly what it said it was and sounded heaps better – but this sort of thing must have been happening all the time. Valuable instruments and artworks would have been hidden in the hope of them surviving the war, only to be claimed later and found to have been replaced by fakes – or else they would have vanished into thin air, like the family's grand piano, which obviously must have existed at some point, and possibly still does somewhere.

The economic problems were severe. Gustav feared he wouldn't be able to get another job at his age, quite apart from being Jewish. Despite the problems, the government still needed skilled people so he did eventually manage to find an engineering job with the Ministry of Works. As a government employee, he had the right to wear a smaller star than the rest of the family – about 5cm across, rather than the usual 10cm. Was he somehow less Jewish now that he was a government employee? It would be laughable if the implications weren't so horrific. He was now deemed employable due to being designated an 'economically necessary Jew', but his salary was dismally low as there was a strict limit on what a Jew could earn, however economically necessary they might be.

Now that Gustav was back in work, with a regular if stingy salary, the family had greater financial stability for a while. In January 1940, they moved from the large apartment to *Coburg*, a smaller modern apartment in a block of flats overlooking the bridge across the river Danube. Their flat was on the third floor of a five or six storey block, and was comfortable enough, but the location made sleep difficult. Ammunition-filled trains rumbled through the night making an awful noise which would take some getting used to after the quiet apartment overlooking the park. The flat itself was serviceable if not luxurious. It had three main rooms, a kitchen and bathroom, central heating and constant hot water. The windows were huge and took up a whole wall, giving plenty of natural light. The situation was convenient enough as the Jewish school was only about half an hour's walk away through the town.

It was during this time that Gustav was suddenly taken ill with acute abdominal pains. Kamila rang for an ambulance but was told there would be a long delay as all the hospitals were full. She said Gustav would happily go to the Jewish hospital. The ambulance came straight away. Nobody wanted to go to the Jewish hospital so there was no problem with overcrowding and no queuing. There was a good reason for this hospital's lack of popularity. Patients feared they would be deported if they identified so obviously as being Jewish, and were all gathered together in one place, so they did anything they could to avoid being an in-patient. Jana doesn't know exactly what the medical problem was, but thinks Gustav must have been having an attack of gall stones or possibly a strangulated hernia, as he suffered from both at one time or another. In the event, he was safely and promptly treated at the hospital and able to return home.

Despite the political situation and the closing of borders, the family was managing to keep some contact with Jirka. This was thanks to one of their maids from the old apartment. She lived on the other side of the Danube, in what was now part of Germany, but crossed the river every day in order to work in Bratislava. She had a daughter, a little younger than Jana, and they would sometimes play together but the daughter was learning the old-fashioned Gothic German way of writing so Jana found pencil and paper games with her tricky. This little girl did speak fluent Slovak, however, so they managed well enough with other forms of play. As the mother was able to cross the border so easily for work, she could keep the family in touch with Jirka by posting their letters and parcels to him from within Germany, something which wouldn't have been possible from Slovakia. At Christmas she brought the family a particularly special present from Jirka – a 78rpm record of him playing one of Liszt's *Hungarian Rhapsodies* for piano. This record was played by the family over and over again until it finally became worn out with overuse. In return, Kamila was able to send Jirka homemade cakes, dried fruit and chocolate. These ingredients were still available in Slovakia, but she knew he wouldn't have been able to obtain them in Prague.

Jirka could not have been living in a worse place at that time, but he now had no choice; there was no way of leaving in safety. Uncle Leo and Aunt Rézi, with whom he had been living, were among the first wave of Jews to be deported from Prague. They were transported to the Łódź Ghetto, where conditions were appalling. The Jews and Roma in the ghetto were entirely dependent on the German authorities for food and medication and were being systematically starved. Overcrowding and forced labour on too little sustenance led to frequent epidemics. Aunt Rézi died of there of typhus. Her husband Leo became one of the leaders of the ghetto, but he never returned, so he must have perished there too.

Jirka had escaped this wave of deportation somehow and was now staying with Uncle Otto and Aunt Milada, also in Prague. The family never found out why he had gone to live with them rather than with Uncle Viktor and his wife Aunt Miluška. Viktor and Miluška's son, Miloš, had always been great friends with Jirka, so it would have seemed more logical for them to take him in, but for whatever reason, they couldn't. There's a temptation is to say, that if he'd gone there, he would have been safe – but the converse is also true as if he'd gone there, it's possible that none of them would have been safe. Viktor's family may have remained safe because of his work, but there's no way of knowing. In the event, Uncle Otto, Aunt Milada and Jirka were all deported. They were transported to Minsk, in Belarus, along with many others from Bohemia and Moravia. The three of them were among the thousands massacred at Maly Trostenets extermination camp, a few miles east of Minsk. Maly Trostenets had originally been built as a Soviet concentration camp to house prisoners of war, but by May 1942 it had become a Nazi extermination camp. Most Jews transported there met their deaths immediately on arrival. By the time the Red Army retook the city in July 1944, the Nazis had blown the place up in an attempt to destroy the evidence, but the grave pits were soon found. Of the tens of thousands taken there, only two Jews remained alive,.and only one of them survived beyond the end of the war.

Years later, Viktor's son Miloš named his firstborn daughter, Jiřina (Georgina), in memory of his friend and cousin, Jirka (Jiři/George). Some years ago, Miloš and his two children, Jiřina and her younger brother Viktor, came to England and we all had a holiday together, along with Pavel and his wife Ruth, in the unlikely setting of Cromer, on the Norfolk coast. My recollections of Miloš are of a friendly and cheerful cousin of my mother's. In more recent times, my mother and Jiřina have taken some holidays together, so the close family ties continue.

Gustav and Kamila were not able to stay in their shiny new apartment with its picture windows for very long. This may have been because the owners of the block were becoming wary – even scared – of having Jewish tenants, or it may have been, as Pavel has suggested, that a Nazi had decided he fancied the flat for himself. Whatever the reason, the family was soon on the move again. Jana was sorry to leave as she had become friendly with Eva Linhartová, a girl of her own age in the flat beneath their own. Eva spent a lot of time in Jana's flat as the two girls had decided to make a dolls' house together. This consisted of cardboard boxes which they painted and furnished with matchboxes, carved conkers and toothpicks, with homemade curtains and knitted carpets. Much later on, Jana discovered that Eva had been Fedor Čermák's first girlfriend – Jirka's old playmate from the original apartment over the showroom.

Occasionally the two girls were joined by Jana's clever friend from the Jewish school, Vera Schlesingerová, but this never really worked out as Vera's jealously always got in the way. She wanted to be Jana's exclusive friend. When her family moved from Bratislava to a village near Nitra, Jana was invited across in the school holidays. This was after she had been baptised, so she was known there as Vera's 'Goy' friend. Vera had a crush from afar on the son of the family who lived in the local manor. She hoped one day to meet him but knew it was unlikely as he was of the nobility and a Catholic and she was a Jewish nobody. Jana couldn't understand her feelings as at that time she had yet to develop any sort of romantic interest in boys.

Jana's family vacated their apartment in a hurry at the end of 1941. The notice given was too short to find anywhere else straight away, but the Ehrensteins, friends from the old stamp collecting days, came to the rescue. They had just enough room in their house to accommodate them while they looked for alternative accommodation. The Ehrensteins lived about 5km north-east of central Bratislava in a district called *Tehelné Pole*, which translates as 'brickyard'. Nowadays, much of the area is an uninspiring wasteland where buildings have been demolished, next to modern-looking factories and office blocks, everything being overlooked by mean looking blocks of flats. At least it had a football stadium, not that that would have meant much to Jana at the time. She has vague memories of its construction, but that is all. Bratislava had lost most of its sporting facilities at this time, but the new stadium was being built from 1939 onwards, and was officially opened in 1941. Later on it would become the home ground for the Czechoslovak national team, and is now a major attraction due to a continual programme of enlargement and improvement. Jana had no interest in football, but does remember the nearby swimming pool, where the local boys would take advantage of the highest diving tower to watch football matches without needing tickets.

Conditions were cramped at the Ehrenstein's, but at least the family had somewhere safe and secure to live for the time being. They had to share one bed-sitting room between the four of them, and had the use of the kitchen and bathroom. While they were there, Mr Ehrenstein taught Jana a German communist song, which led her to believe he must have been a communist himself. He also lent her a 'Teach Yourself Russian' book. At all the schools she had attended so far, the children had been forced to learn German, so in her quiet rebellious way she was delighted to be able to teach herself some Russian. I think she must have picked this up very well, despite its difficulties, because when I was little I'm sure I remember a row of Russian books on a shelf at home – literary classics like Chekhov stories and Pushkin poems. I asked her about this recently and she said though she still knows enough Russian to follow a story, she can't speak it with any confidence. As far as German is concerned, she's currently attending German language classes, so her objections to learning the language obviously no longer apply.

The situation at the Ehrensteins couldn't continue indefinitely. Both families would have to move out of Bratislava shortly, and everything would change yet again. Most importantly, on a personal level, Jana was soon to meet a young girl who was destined to become a lifelong friend.

13

GERDA

In March 1942, just two months after Jana and her family had come to stay with them, the Ehrensteins had to move out of the city and into the village of Lamač, about 8k north-west of central Bratislava. It could have been worse. Lamač at this time was still a village, rather than the suburb it has since become, and was independent of the city. The area was famous for its vineyards, and useful for supplying produce to the Bratislava markets. The main railway line ran through the village, so commuting into central Bratislava was perfectly feasible for the residents. The village had been rebuilt after being burnt to the ground during the final battle of the Austro-Prussian War in July 1866, so there were no old or distinguished buildings other than the pretty seventeenth century Chapel of Saint Rozalia which had luckily escaped the conflagration.

The Ehrensteins moved into a house that had been divided into two flats. The occupants of the other part of the house were Hugo Kaufmann, his wife Ilona, and their twin daughters Gerda and Vera. Jews were very restricted in their movements by now and only allowed to live in certain areas, so the Kaufmann family, like the Grafs and the Ehrensteins, had been downsizing, forced to sell larger items of furniture and leave more central locations. Hugo Kaufmann was an old friend of the Grafs. He ran a philately shop in Bratislava so he and Gustav had known each other for years through their shared interest in stamps. Jana had first come across Hugo's twin daughters when all three girls were attending the Jewish school in Bratislava, but as Jana was two years older than the twins, she had stuck to friends of her own age at that time. Later, things would change, and circumstances would throw Gerda and Jana together in a way which neither could have predicted.

Gerda and Vera were non-identical twins, very different to each other in every way. Their mother, Ilona, liked to dress them more or less the same, but with subtle differences to match their temperaments, so they might were identical style dresses, but in different colours with matching ribbons braided into their hair. Gerda was tall and slim, with light brown wavy hair, so might wear blue, while Vera was short, giggly and lively, with very dark hair and more likely to be dressed in red. Gerda was as quiet as Vera was boisterous and argumentative, so when they eventually became friends, Jana naturally gravitated towards the quieter Gerda.

The twins had grown up speaking German and Hungarian at home, but Slovak to their maid and neighbours. Their parents had gradually started speaking more and more Slovak at home themselves to prepare the girls for school. The Kaufmann's were a happy, normal family in every way, and I am very grateful to Gerda for having provided many details of the family's home life – small things that at the time feel unimportant, but which later on evoke a time and a place far more than historical facts and figures can do. At breakfast time, for example, the girls would greet the adults with a respectful 'good morning' and eat thinly sliced bread spread with honey or strawberry jam, while their father, Hugo, poured out cocoa for everyone. Mealtimes were always pleasant affairs, though any bursts of laughter from the girls would be met with reproving looks from one or other of the adults. Although they had a maid, the girls still helped with the lighter household chores as a matter of principle. They would later look back at this happy time with a curious nostalgia – like so many others, they could not possibly have known how dramatically everything was about to change.

100

Their early childhood was very similar to Jana's own. A favourite trip in the summer would be to take the short tram ride to their grandfather's orchard where they would pick cherries, hanging the twin-stemmed fruit from the ears as earrings. On very hot days they went swimming in the Danube in the open air swimming pool, not far from their grandfather's orchard on the south side of Bratislava. This pool – or lido – was a wooden structure with a platform and two sets of steps leading into the fast flowing river. The changing rooms were on the riverbank. Gerda was always sure the fast flowing current would sweep her through the wooden slits or under the stairs, so she preferred to sit on the steps and paddle her feet, ignoring the calls of 'Coward!' from her sister. On rainy or cooler days they amused themselves at home. They had use of a record player, and as they initially lived in a substantial two storey house, they didn't have to worry about disturbing their parents or anyone else.

During this time they had frequent visits from various relations. Their paternal grandmother was a favourite. She who owned a big black coat which the girls thought made her look like a friendly grizzly bear. Gerda was particularly struck by the coat because of the stark contrast the yellow star made upon it; the badge that turned her into an outsider, dehumanised her, made her into a *persona non grata*. The twins didn't understand the significance of the star at the time, but Gerda noticed how her grandmother wore her handbag in an attempt to conceal the star, even though this was strictly against the rules. The old lady was almost certainly wearing her friendly 'grizzly bear' coat when she was later deported to Auschwitz.

The twins' maternal grandparents were far more strict and earnest and considered laughter to be a sign of ill-breeding. When the twins visited them, they had to remain silent unless spoken to – and if they spoke, it had to be in German. At the table, they had to hold a book under each arm so that their elbows wouldn't stick out. Everything was about correction. Gerda coped pretty well with the regime

101

and was happy to do as she was told, but the livelier Vera found it all too ridiculous and would often break into giggles, and then not understand why the adults got so cross with her. These grandparents were called by the German words *Omama* and *Opapa*, but their paternal grandmother was known by the gentler sounding Slovak word: *babička*.

Like so many in their situation, the downsizing would soon become inevitable and the family was forced to make a series of moves to smaller and smaller apartments, further away from the centre of Bratislava. All the time, their friends and relatives were mysteriously disappearing. Hugo and Ilona would whisper together, trying to protect their daughters, from the situation, so they were left in the dark as to exactly what was happening – very like Jana's own experience of lying awake at night, listening to hushed discussions, being scared and not knowing what was going on. Gerda used to say she wished she could erase the memories of this time.

Their Kaufmann's first move was to a fifth floor flat in Štefániková Street, where the trams rattled by just outside the window. This flat had a balcony all along the front and the girls used to hang on the railings, daring each other to see who could lean over the furthest. They didn't stay at this flat for very long before they had to move again, this time to a much quieter house on a steep hill called Holubyho Ulica. This location was ideal for sledging on winter Sundays, a sport which Vera loved but Gerda hated. Her father made her join in as he thought it would be character-building, but she was as nervous about sledging as she had been about swimming in the river.

The Kaufmann family were some of the earliest to be christened, while Jana and her family were some of the last. Unlike Gustav, Hugo Kaufmann had taken the theological aspect of the procedure very seriously and had engaged Pastor Lasdislav Jurkovič to give private lessons to Gerda and Vera. The girls were already familiar with much of the Old Testament, so it was the Pastor's job to explain to them the Protestant faith, the significance of the parables, and what the story of Jesus meant to Christians. They would have seen the nativity scenes that were displayed in front of the municipal theatre every Christmas, but had probably never thought much about what happened to that baby when he grew up. The pastor was a kindly man and did his best to make the change of religion as painless as possible, but the girls were fully aware that this was a pretence. They couldn't believe in this new religion and knew they were having to learn it in order to fool the authorities. They were used to considering themselves to be part of an enlightened section of society, but now they had to lie; their whole culture and identity had to be hidden. They dutifully did as they were told and completed their course of instruction, were baptized in the church, and received the official documentation attesting to their status as members of the Lutheran church. The authorities knew this sort of thing was going on, so the chances of it working were slim, but for the time being it gave a small illusion of safety.

Mrs Kaufmann later told Kamila she strongly believed children should be brought up in a religion, but it didn't matter which one. This was the only disagreement the two women ever had, as far as Jana can recall.

In many ways the Kaufmann's lives were following a similar pattern to Jana's family, with the sudden drop in income, the necessity to downsize, and the crazy restrictions in what they could do and where they could live. Two men in overalls came to their flat one day and measured all the furniture. Gerda and her sister had been sent to their room to do their homework, but they were curious, and listened to find out what was going on. Their parents were discussing the furniture – whether they really needed some of the larger items, like the display cabinet, which in Gerda's view was a nuisance anyway as far as the maid was concerned because of all the extra shelves to dust. Her mother, however, was clearly attached to this object, and when Gerda asked about it later, Ilona, clearly upset, explained that however much she wanted to keep it, the cabinet was too big and would have to go as they were moving to a much smaller flat.

A few days later they went to see the new place. It was on another steep hill, and worse than that, in Gerda's eyes it was close to derelict – neglected, with peeling plaster, and an unkempt yard of bare earth and scruffy grass rather than a garden. Gerda had to be dragged through the gate, but she cheered up when she saw the rabbit hutch containing two rabbits. She stroked the animals, loving the feel of their soft fur. Within minutes a housekeeper had come out of the house and pushed her away – it turned out the rabbits belonged to her son, and were out of bounds for Gerda, however much she wanted to pet them. It later transpired that the rabbits were given more carrots to eat than the Kaufmann's entire allocation.

Gerda never approached the animals again, despite the temptation. The smell of the rabbit hutch stayed in her nostrils the whole time the family lived in the house, mingled with the odour of dampness. The front of the house might have been okay, but Gerda and family occupied the smaller rooms in the back which remained dark and miserable despite Hugo's efforts to brighten them up with a fresh lick of paint.

Hostility towards Jews was steadily increasing at this time and the girls were always aware of people whispering behind their backs. Their sense of security was gone, mostly due to the constant threat of imminent moves and the arbitrary and unreasonable rules they had to follow. Their landlord didn't help matters with his frequent anti-Semitic remarks, and the whole family was worried that he might hand them over to the authorities. The hated Hlinka Guard patrolled the street regularly and would peer into people's faces in an intimidating manner. Unfortunately, many of the residents of the street approved of this behaviour – or perhaps they thought it safest to appear to approve. Whatever the reasons, many of the houses started to fly the Slovak national flag. The area was fast becoming a Nationalist stronghold.

As the situation deteriorated, Hugo Kaufmann was forced to give up his philately shop on Venturska Street. His name was erased from the shop front as the hostility grew. He could no longer produce the stamp catalogues that used to bear his name, but managed to find work thanks to a friend who offered him a job with the Tekla printing company in a nearby town. His friend was taking a risk in giving employment to a Jew, but this work enabled Hugo to pay the bills and also to have his stamp catalogues issued under a pseudonym His wife meanwhile had managed to get a secretarial post in a government office – the Ministry of Commerce – thanks to her skills in shorthand, typing and her fluency in three languages. This work should have given the family exemption from deportation, but nothing could be relied upon any more. If the authorities couldn't locate the names on their lists for deportation, they would take anyone else randomly to make up the numbers. Ilona always arranged for Vera and Gerda to sleep at separate friends' houses on nights when it looked like deportation was likely, and she tried to ensure the girls were never visible when a police patrol was in the area.

Hugo didn't dare go out in the evenings because of his obviously Semitic features, so it would be the girls' mother who would take them round to friends' houses. The twins wouldn't be told in advance that this was going to happen, though on one occasion when Vera asked what was going on, her mother explained that people might come and take them to the ghetto, and they didn't want that. Hugo and Ilona would often argue about the situation – she was sure the exemption rules couldn't possibly keep them safe, but he was all for obeying orders as it went against the grain for him not to do so. Nobody knew what was really going on, but the rumours of what happened to people who were being deported were terrifying. The Kaufmanns knew they were going to have to find a better way to keep the girls safe.

Eventually, sleeping in other people's homes was no longer an option. They had to move to another house, where they were effectively hiding. It was no longer possible to live openly in any safety, so they moved to the outskirts of Lamač, where they lived in a house surrounded by neglected fences and an assortment of hens. The twins and their family had one room for sleeping and living in, and shared the kitchen and bathroom with their landlady, a friendly lady called Mrs Pernicova. Gerda was glad to be away from the previous street, with their unpleasant landlord and his complaining son. The girls didn't exactly drop out of school at this point, but the bus stop was a three kilometre walk from the house, so they went less and less often, and just attended enough to enable them to pass exams. Their mother was able to pick up homework for them, and they also had a private teacher who gave them various lessons, including French, but the situation was unsatisfactory, and for much of the week the girls would be idle and quarrelsome.

There was always talk of the war, but the twins didn't exactly feel at war – where they were living, there were no bombs and no shooting. Life was strange, with the constant moving, but they had been insulated by their parents from the worst of what was really going on. The realisation that this was not how things should be only crept up on them gradually.

Soon they were on the move again, away from the secluded house on the main road. They packed up the few pieces of furniture that they still owned, leaving behind a favourite cupboard, and moved into the middle of the village of Lamač, into a tiny house with a strip of garden with some straggly old roses. In the winter, the north facing wall of the house was covered in a sheet of ice. The house itself was bitterly cold as they had no access to a heating allowance – and no food allowance either. When the snow what at its heaviest, Hugo dug a tunnel through it to make a path to the front door. This sounds grim, but for the imaginative Gerda, the ice tunnel made it feel as if she was living in a fairy tale, and because of the insulating snow, the tunnel was actually warmer than the house itself.

By this time, Jews were no longer allowed to swim in the common pools, to skate on common ground, or to use normal public transport. The girls couldn't indulge in any sports, and spent their time watched over by a succession of child-minders, none of whom stayed very long.

One fateful evening, there was a knock at the door – Hugo was handed some papers and told to pack. He was taken to Sered labour camp. In desperation, Ilona contacted all her friends in the government, trying to find some way to free him. A few weeks later, miraculously, he was able to return to them, bruised, beaten and thinner. He never said much about those times, but it was clear that he had only just escaped being deported from Seren to one of the concentration camps.

Ilona now made it very clear to the girls that they were not to leave the house under any circumstances. The girls, however, were often desperate to get out, and did sneak away every so often, always being very careful, and never speaking to anyone. One particularly vivid memory for Gerda was an occasion when she was standing by the side of the road as a long line of women walked past, most of them young, each carrying a suitcase. They all wore the yellow star. Every woman looked at the one in front with a glazed expression that chilled Gerda. She later described the silence after they'd all gone by as a horrible scream.

14

ACCIDENTAL MUSHROOMS

Once the Ehrensteins knew they were going to move to Lamač, Jana's family had to sort out their own new accommodation pretty quickly. They managed to find a place in Dúbravka, a village of about 5000 inhabitants on the south-west side of Lamač. The facilities in this house were very basic. There was no indoor bathroom or toilet, so the family had to make do with an outdoor privy. This was essentially a hole in the ground, though it had a wooden structure above it to give a bit of shelter. When water was required for drinking, cooking or washing, this had to be collected from a well by lowering a bucket on a rope as there was no pump available.

I have to keep reminding myself that this was a family whose original bathroom had boasted a state of the art shower attachment with instant hot water; who had used the latest model washing machine; who had surrounded themselves with fine art – carefully selected contemporary paintings by Slovak artists; beautiful examples of Czech glasswork; Dresden figurines. This was the family where everyone played the piano and sang, and yes, they could still sing in Dúbravka, but I don't imagine they felt like it very often.

Gustav, Kamila, Pavel and Jana were once again crammed into a single bed-sitting room, but at least they had their own kitchen with a wood-burning range, a larder, and a small additional room which was filled with wardrobes. I've no idea why they had a small room filled with wardrobes, but I suppose it gave storage space if nothing else. If anyone wanted to wash properly, a tin bath had to be brought into the kitchen and the water heated on the range in much the same way peasants had managed for centuries. Unlike many other houses in the village, this one was wired for electricity so they had electric light and weren't reliant on oil lamps or candles.

The house in Dúbravka belonged to a man with the surname Brenčič. He was a member of the Hlinka Guard, the hated militia that was maintained by the Slovak People's Party – or in other words, a Nazi in all but name. The Hlinka Guard had been in existence since 1938 as a direct response to the Sudetenland crisis. They lasted until 1945, at which point membership became punishable by five to twenty years' imprisonment. The role was to act as the state police, so they were responsible for operating against Jews, Czechs, Hungarians, the Left and the opposition. They wore black uniforms and a boat-shaped cap with a pompom on top, and used the raised arm salute. Members of the Guard were responsible for the deportations of Slovak Jews to concentration camps and confiscation of their property, which they would generally keep for themselves, which meant many in the higher ranks became very wealthy. To have someone like this as a landlord must have felt very strange, and quite how a member of the Hlinka Guard could bring himself to have Jews living in his house, Jana doesn't know. One can only assume that the opportunity for making money by renting out rooms overcame his ideological convictions and he wasn't too fussed who his tenants were.

The family's rooms were on the ground floor of the house, while Brenčič lived on the upper floor with his wife and their three small sons, Vítek, Milan and Janko, who were aged three to six. Shortly after Jana and family moved in, the Brenčič family had another baby boy, Zdenko. These small boys made a constant nuisance of themselves. The worst was Janko, whom Jana describes as 'a real pest'. He liked to spy through knot holes in the wooden door of the privy hut when anyone was using the facilities. He also peed through the lower holes just for the hell of it, and specialised in knocking over buckets of water that had just been pulled out of the well. Despite the problems with these children, Jana must have made an effort to get on with them because when baby Zdenko was born, she made a baby gown for him at her needlework class in school – this was in pale blue fabric, trimmed with lace, and was the first real garment she had made all by herself. This was the start of a lifelong interest in dressmaking for Jana. She made many of her own clothes, as well as nearly all of mine when I was little, and eventually, years later, became wardrobe mistress for a local amateur dramatics group, the Wickham Court Players, where she won an award for costumes.

One of Jana's abiding memories from this time is of Mr Brenčič playing his saxophone every evening at high volume and with little technique – a minor thing in the overall scheme of things, but for his very musical tenants it must have been painful.

Some of the upstairs rooms in the house were rented by the village school teacher. Gustav and Kamila hoped this lady would be able to give Pavel a better education than the one he was receiving in the local secondary school, so they employed her to supplement his schooling by delivering a more Gymnasium-style education, chiefly in mathematics, a subject in which Pavel would later shine. He also had Latin lessons from the teacher's brother, who was still a student. Collecting water from a well, whilst studying higher mathematics; Latin and tin baths, outside toilets and calculus – this was a question of priorities. Education was something that mattered deeply to this family, and they were going to pursue it even if everything else in their world was collapsing. In the end it paid off, even though at the time a bright future as a mathematician must have seemed an unlikely dream for Pavel. It would never have happened without a combination of Gustav's natural optimism and Kamila's belief, based on family experience, that education is the best route to improve your situation, whatever your circumstances.

At one of Jana's secondary schools in Bratislava, there was a history teacher who refused to teach the history of Europe as prescribed by the Nazis. Instead, he taught the children about the Ancient Romans and Greeks. You can teach a lot about democracy by studying the Greeks, so Jana wonders how he got away with it, but this sort of quiet subversion must have been going on all over the place.

Dúbravka had one general store which sold pretty much everything apart from fresh meat. There was also a butcher, a pub, a midwife, a primary school which had the only telephone in the village, a travelling greengrocer who called at the village once or twice a week, and a Roman Catholic Church and priest. This village priest had no problem with the newcomers, and became good friends with Gustav, even to the extent of showing him photos of his children – which presumably he couldn't have shown any but his most understanding parishioners. Milk was bought directly from the farmers, as was meat from time to time. Word would come around when a pig was due to be slaughtered. The farmer would legally have to give a certain percentage of this meat to the authorities, but the rest could be retained for his own consumption. Rather than saving it all for himself, he naturally sold much of it to anyone willing to pay. Similar rules applied to cow's milk. Goat's milk was not rationed, as presumably a goat would be expected to produce only enough milk for the family that owned it. Milk of any kind wasn't so easily available in central Bratislava, so Jana and Pavel would often take some on the train when they went to school to give to friends in the city who couldn't get any. This was strictly against the law, but they did it anyway. One winter's day when she was collecting the milk, Jana slipped on some ice and fell and hurt her back. Everyone was far more concerned about the spilt milk than her bruised back, which luckily wasn't too seriously hurt.

Gustav and Kamila had some friends who ran a market garden and vineyard in the nearby village of Karlová Ves. A mutual friend of theirs in Dúbravka worked at this market garden and was sometimes able to bring back a basket of produce for the family, so the usual restricted diet caused by the shortages and could be varied. There were other ways of enlivening the diet. Despite all the problems of living at Dúbravka, this was effectively rural living, very different to being in central Bratislava, so countryside foraging was easy and could supplement the meagre rations available from shops. The village was surrounded by farmland and woods, which gave a wealth of opportunities for foraging for berries and mushrooms, as well as flowers to brighten up the house. If the best mushrooms could only be collected by 'accidentally' straying into what was then Germany, this didn't matter, as the border wasn't patrolled in such rural areas. Kamila was particularly knowledgeable about fungi, knowing not only which ones were good to eat, but also the best way of cooking them; which were best for soup, which worked well in pickles, and so on.

Gustav had no interest in nature, but Kamila once persuaded him to accompany them on a ramble saying he would see some magnificent beauty spots. He wasn't enthusiastic, but agreed to come. When they reached a clearing in the woods, he suddenly said, with typical Gustav-style humour 'There's the beauty!' pointing to a corner where a couple was locked in an embrace.

Jana kept in close touch during this period with Gerda and Vera in neighbouring Lamač. The girls would often put on shows together, which might be little dramatic sketches they had written, or scenes from fairy tales interspersed with songs and dances. They wore traditional Slovak embroidered blouses for these, and Mrs Kaufmann made them multi-layered skirts from crepe paper. Their families and neighbours made up the audience. Kamila suggested they should include Pavel as she thought he would be feeling left out, but Jana was then twelve, an age when boys were not wanted, and I doubt if fourteen year old Pavel would have remained interested very long anyway.

During this period, one of their landlord's sons was diagnosed with polio. The village did not have a doctor, so the family asked a retired doctor in a neighbouring village for advice. Pavel was dispatched to fetch the latest serum provided by a laboratory to help prevent infection. Both he and Jana took a dose to safeguard them as they were living in the same house as the infected child. Pavel nearly fainted when he was given his injection. This was possibly not helped by the fact that he'd had no food or drink that day. Luckily he suffered no further side effects. Jana, however, developed a high fever and headache and started passing out. I've looked up these symptoms, and see that in some cases polio infection can cause aseptic meningitis, so I'm guessing this might have been what happened to her. I have no idea what the serum from the laboratory might have been as there was no cure or effective treatment for polio available at this time, so it must have been an experimental treatment of some kind, intended to increase resistance to infection.

Jana was sent to stay with the Ehrensteins in nearby Lamač to recover and avoid any cross-infections. She was much better after a week or two, which again fits in with the possible meningitis diagnosis, as that would have taken two to ten days to run its course. She and Pavel were very lucky that neither caught full-blown polio as the only available treatments for the killer disease were crude and ineffective at that time. A vaccine wouldn't be available for another decade. With no doctor in Dúbravka, Kamila had earned a reputation for being able to cure minor ailments, but obviously she couldn't have done anything about polio. She was, however, very knowledgeable about the medicinal properties of various herbs, such as chamomile water for infantile eczema and bitter aloes – which Jana found truly disgusting – for stomach cramps.

On one occasion Pavel fell ill with a severe middle ear infection which spread to the bone behind the ear. Kamila realised he would need hospital treatment for this, so Gustav contacted Mr Muzikář, who had helped them out with family trips back the days when they lived in the old apartment. He was happy to do a bit of chauffeuring, and offered to drive Pavel and Kamila to the hospital in Bratislava – though he wasn't impressed by the unmade muddy roads of Dúbravka and commented that a couple of buckets of concrete wouldn't come amiss. Pavel's ear infection proved to be serious, as suspected, and he had to have part of the bone removed. Luckily the operation was a success and pretty much sorted out the problem. Kamila stayed in Bratislava with some friends during this time so that she could visit Pavel daily in hospital – this was most likely the Jewish hospital.

While her mother and Pavel were away, Jana had to take over looking after her father. She was around thirteen years old at this time. Gustav couldn't cook at all, so would have been helpless with nobody around to sort him out. He could make coffee and boil an egg, but that was it. Jana's job would have been simple enough, had it not been for the restrictions that were in force. You couldn't simply pop down the corner shop for a loaf of bread. Bread or bread flour was rationed, and you had to opt for one or the other, so Kamila had always opted for flour. Jana didn't know what to do with it, but their landlady helped out by showing her how to make sourdough rye bread. After the first disastrous attempt, she became reasonably proficient at making up the dough. This was put in a special basket and taken to the village baker who had a brick oven in which all the village bread was baked. In the afternoon she would return to the bakery to fetch the freshly baked loaves. She still makes the occasional loaf of bread to this day, though now of course she bakes it herself.

This was a strange time – a time of waiting, of not knowing. The family had a roof over their heads, they were all together, they had food, but they were also under enormous stress. They had settled into a basic sort of rural living, but each time anything in their situation changed, it changed for the worse. They must have wondered how long this could continue; how bad things could possibly become before they got better – if they got better.

15

HAYSTACKS

The previous lodgings at Lamač had been conveniently close to the railway line to Bratislava, but the house in Dúbravka was about half an hour's walk through the village to the railway halt. This was no problem for the children, but Gustav hated it. He was emphatically not a walker, but had no choice but to walk in all weathers to get to work. The children had to use the railway line to catch the train to their schools in Bratislava. These trains were steam locomotives which pulled the old-fashioned style of carriages with uncovered ends that one sees in Wild West films – what would technically be called balcony bogie coaches. When the carriages were full, the children had to stand on the uncovered balconies at the end. This was fine except for the tunnels which inevitably filled with smoke as the trains passed through. When even the carriage ends were full, the children tried to stand on the steps but this was, quite rightly, not allowed on safety grounds. The guard had to tell them to get off, which meant they had to wait for the next train which made them late for school. Teachers can be very unsympathetic, so to solve the problem of the lateness, the station master was very accommodating and always gave the children a note to explain why they hadn't been allowed on the train that would have got them there on time. Needless to say, the children exploited the situation, making sure they arrived at the station at the very last minute so they were prevented from travelling due to overcrowding.

This arrangement hadn't been going on very long when they were forced to change schools yet again. Jana had been doing very well at the Jewish school. The last two school reports, ending in 1942, gave 1s in every subject, but she couldn't stay there as out of town pupils were now barred from attending school in Bratislava because of the dangers of air raids. As a result, Jana and Pavel had to attend a small rural school in Devínska Nová Ves, about an hour's walk across fields and lanes. Jana continued to impress her teachers as is evident from the first report from this new school, which dispensed with the numbering system, but used the word *výborný* (excellent) for every subject.

I'm sure the walk to the school in Devínska Nová Ves was more pleasant, certainly when the weather was fine, than the train ride through smut-filled tunnels had been. The lanes were lined with cherry trees, which were pretty in the spring and laden with fruit later on. The fields themselves were less interesting, as they were sown with wheat and other cereal crops rather than carrying livestock. The children had to cross a stream en route, but this was no problem as they would be walking barefoot. Shoes were difficult to come by and had to be looked after carefully, so they would take advantage of the stream to wash their feet before entering the village with socks and shoes on.

I've had a look at the satellite view of the area. The direct route from Dúbravka to Devínska Nová Ves goes through thick woodland, so it looks as if the children must have skirted around the northern side, making the walk that little bit longer across what still looks like a largely featureless landscape of large fields with cereal crops. About five children made the daily trek to this school from Dúbravka. Sometimes a few of them would manage to cadge a lift part of the way home on a horse-drawn hay cart, but most of the time they had to walk

The school made use of an old farmhouse rather than having purpose built classrooms. The most memorable lesson for Jana was PE, which was held in a passage way. This would normally have been one of her favourite subjects, but at this school the PE mistress was something of a sadist. If the children didn't ache all over after lessons, the teacher would be disappointed and think they hadn't tried hard enough. She sounds a bit like one or two PE teachers I've known in my time – which is unfair, of course. I'm sure my PE teachers were lovely. I just hated the subject. Jana enjoyed anything to do with physical exercise normally, so I'm sure there really was a problem with these lessons.

In winter, when the school had to close because of fuel shortages, Kamila sent Jana to the local dressmaker Mrs Krebsová to make herself useful and make sure she was still learning something. Similarly, Pavel helped out at a carpenter's and later at a radio shop. The dressmaker and her brother lived on the edge of the village and owned a German shepherd guard dog which would bark loudly whenever anyone passed the house. Jana and her family often spent the evening at the dressmaker's house at it was the only place they could hear the BBC broadcasts. These were the most reliable source of news as regards world events. If the dog started barking, the radio was quickly changed to a different station, known jokingly as *Radio Kroměříž*. This was the name of a town in Bohemia, but with a slightly different spelling the word could also mean 'outside the Reich'. One evening, the dog started barking hysterically. The house owner looked out in a panic to see who it was, but then said with relief, 'It's okay, it's only the policeman coming to listen to the BBC – he can't do it at the police station.' They later heard that this same policeman had joined the partisans in the mountains.

Jana was never going to live anywhere very long without making friends, and in the village she found herself drawn to a girl called Olga Milošovičová. The two of them didn't have much in common as Olga wasn't very academic, but she was terrific fun and had an excellent musical ear. This showed itself in her ability to harmonise immediately if someone started singing a melody. Her father used to cut up bread and put it into his mug of coffee for breakfast, eating it with a spoon, a practice which struck Jana as very odd at the

117

time. She knew about this strange habit because she was sometimes at their house for breakfast. Olga had started inviting her to sleep over in her parent's hay loft above their cottage in the summer, and Gustav and Kamila encouraged this, telling Jana it would be fun. She later realised the real reason her parents approved was to keep her away from home at night which was the time when Jews were usually picked up to be deported. Eventually Olga's parents became frightened by the risks involved in harbouring this Jewish child in their hayloft, and Jana was no longer made welcome.

Gustav and Kamila were desperate to save their children, even if they couldn't save themselves. Gustav was an eternal optimist who thought they would manage to get through it all somehow. I think he was maybe a bit like Hugo in this, who always thought that so long as you followed the rules, everything would be all right. Their wives were more pragmatic. Gustav even hoped to join the Slovak partisans, but when he applied he was told they wouldn't take him as he was too old. Kamila was a realist, and as such was becoming increasingly distraught at the situation, especially after Jirka's disappearance which must have been unbearable. To find some solace, she turned to Judaism and began to keep *Yom Kippur* – something she had never done before, and something which Gustav probably couldn't comprehend.

More and more of their friends had now been deported, including those who had been baptised, so in 1944 the entire family took to sleeping at night on a haystack in a barn that was owned by the farmer from whom they were buying milk. The authorities only came for Jews at night, so they thought this would be safer than staying at home and risking the hammering on the door. They walked to the haystack at different times through the evening, each taking different routes rather than going as a family together at that would have made them too conspicuous.

118

Daytime activities were becoming increasingly difficult because of the increasing restrictions. By this time, Jews were not allowed to own a radio; they couldn't have any sporting equipment such as skis or tennis rackets; and they were only allowed a minimal amount of clothing, so a woman would be allowed a winter coat plus a spring coat or a spring suit, but she couldn't have both the spring coat and the suit. The ever resourceful Kamila found ways round this. She owned a suit with a jacket and button through skirt, which should have counted as two items, but when the authorities came round to inspect and check her wardrobe, she unbuttoned the skirt and laid it out flat on the bed as a fake blanket. She got away with the subterfuge and the skirt wasn't confiscated.

There were many other petty restrictions. Wherever you lived, you had to have a permit to go to the next town or village. Gustav was allowed to travel to Bratislava as it was his workplace, but if Kamila wanted to go into Bratislava for shopping, she had to get a permit to allow this. The village where they lived didn't have an office that could issue permits, so she had to break the law and walk into the next village to get the permit in the first place.

Gustav remained optimistic for as long as he could, but events would finally overtake him and neither his positive thinking nor Kamila's prayers were going to prove effective in the end. This was the last time they would all be together as a family, and there was absolutely nothing any of them could do about it. Some months earlier, Hugo and Ilona Kaufmann had found a way to hide their daughters, Gerda and Vera. It was now time for Gustav and Kamila to take a similar drastic step.

16

GERDA'S GOODBYE TO CHILDHOOD

Gerda's parents had decided that the villages round Bratislava could no longer provide safe hiding places for the family as to stay together as one unit. Their approach was to split up and find the best solutions for each of them. Hugo Kaufmann was able to stay in a small room in the Tekla factory, thanks to his friend Pan Janoš who had arranged for him to work there. The room was kept locked and the other employees didn't even know he was using it. In consultation with Pastor Jurkovič, who had baptised the family, it was decided that it would be best for Gerda and Vera to be placed in an orphanage, as gentiles. Pastor Jurkovič advised them that the girls would be safer in a rural Protestant orphanage rather than a Catholic one in the town. He told them that he was friendly with the pastor in a village called Modra, and this pastor was the supervisor of a boarding school for girls as well as the orphanage which was within walking distance of the school. The orphanage itself should be able to provide a safe haven for the girls. Ilona and Hugo were glad to hear there was a school so close, as the girls hadn't been able to attend regular schooling for the best part of a year.

Gerda and Vera weren't at all convinced by the arguments, but were persuaded that this was for the best. Their mother told them they would have friends again and would be able to study; they wouldn't be on their own any more. The girls didn't know what to say at first, but Gerda was sure she didn't want to go – she was desperate to stay with her mother, though she didn't dare say so. The two of them had always been very close and Gerda didn't think she would be able to bear the separation. The more independent Vera felt more positive about the situation and decided she was happy to try it out. She told Gerda it was just for school term time, after all, and then they would come back home.

The decision was made. The girls packed one suitcase each with clothes, books and toiletries. They travelled by bus to Modra, a journey that took forever as the bus stopped at every little village, passing through sleepy vineyards and clusters of houses that felt as if the war had passed them by entirely. They left the bus at Modra and went directly to Pastor Julius Derer's house. He understood their predicament perfectly, and was ready to help any Jewish child in this situation – he had already done so with several others.

He showed the girls and their mother round both the boarding school and the orphanage so that they could decide which would be more appropriate. The boarding school was a smart building, well looked after, large, but not so large as to be intimidating. The orphanage had a different atmosphere entirely. From the outside, it looked fine, but Gerda's opinion of it changed as soon as a nun unlocked an old heavy door and let them into a vast stone-flagged hall. Gerda decided the broad staircase opposite the entrance must lead to hell rather than heaven.

The pastor introduced them to the nun, Sister Žofia, as 'Vera and Gerda, and Mrs Kaufmann'. He pointedly did not say 'the girls' mother'. Mrs Kaufmann went to another room to talk to Sister Žofia while Gerda and Vera stood in the chilly hall, which felt much colder than outside. Their suitcases stood next to them on the floor. Gerda thought the cases looked like orphans too.

Their mother returned. It was decided. The girls would stay here, in the orphanage, rather than the boarding school. Pastor Derer asked Sister Žofia to enrol them. He said goodbye, and the nun took the girls and their mother up to a dormitory in which identical beds stood in four long

121

rows. She pointed to two beds, said 'The girls will sleep here, Mrs Kaufmann', and walked away, without giving anyone a chance to say or ask anything.

Vera and Gerda stood there, bemused. Gerda begged her mother to let them at least stay in the boarding school, but Ilona explained they would be more secure among the orphans. In the boarding school, people would get curious about girls whose parents never visited, but that wouldn't be an issue in the orphanage. Gerda realised this meant her mother would not be visiting them, and she was about to complain about this when her mother explained that the girls must not reveal that they had living parents. They had to keep this secret. 'Only the Pastor and the Sister in charge of the orphanage know that you have parents and are Jewish,' she said. Then she gave them a hug and took two little gold chains with crosses out of her handbag and put them round the girls' necks. 'Never take them off,' she said, 'and remember, when asked, that you are Protestant.' Both girls followed these instructions to the letter and kept the chains until after the war.

Their mother unpacked their things and put them away into the little lockers by the sides of their beds. That was it. One last goodbye, and she was gone. Neither girl cried. Between them, they managed to make believe that the situation wasn't terrible, but Gerda felt her childhood had come to an end. She and her sister were on their own, utterly. At eleven years old, they could no longer rely on their parents or even their own names. They were without identity, forced to lie. Gerda couldn't help wondering if she would ever see her mother again.

The orphanage was housed in a large nineteenth century building divided into wings for groups of orphans of different ages. Gerda's abiding impression was of an unfriendly and alienating environment, with many massive rooms which were freezing in winter. The dormitory in which Gerda and Vera were sleeping had four rows of identical beds in precise, straight lines. The beds were of white painted metal and looked like hospital beds. The only difference between each individual bed was the random pattern of grey patches where the paint had peeled away. Each girl had a small locker in which she was allowed to keep toiletries and spare underwear, but that was it. They were not allowed any private belongings. Their uniform dresses were kept by the nuns, who distributed them with little consideration for size as far as Gerda could tell. They were allocated a clean uniform once a week after they'd taken turns to wash in the same bath tub.

The girls all wore flannel dresses, with slightly varying geometric patterns. Stockings were patched cotton, often torn, with bare knees showing in the older girls, but not in the younger as the dresses often reached down to their ankles. Gerda felt like a scarecrow, and thought everyone else looked just as bad.

The weekly bath was a torment. Hot water was no doubt in short supply, but the water got colder and dirtier as the line of girls waiting for their bath progressed. This allowed for easy transmission of skin diseases and lice. The girls never asked the nuns why they all had to take a bath on the same day, but each week they'd complain amongst themselves.

Everyone caught colds in the winter so Sister Anna handed out large cotton handkerchiefs to them all. These had to be laundered by the girls every few hours by rinsing them through in cold water and then gluing them onto the warm tiles of the stoves that heated the classroom to dry. Each time was done, the handkerchief grew stiffer.

The dining room was for Gerda a different kind of torture. This huge room was filled with long tables, with girls at some and boys at others. There was a dais at one end with a boxwood table for the nuns. There was plenty of food, which Vera loved, but it made the more sensitive Gerda gag. Vera helped her out by wolfing down anything Gerda really couldn't stomach. Gerda played with her food, arranging the beans in rows like the beds in the dormitories, and decorating each with a grain of something she describes as 'grout' – some sort of cereal, presumably. She absolutely hated 'grout' and couldn't swallow it, not even when it was used to thicken a tasty tomato soup.

The nuns used their dais as a punishment area. For a mild offence, such as a poor school mark or minor insolence, the child would be given a few lashes on an outstretched palm. For stealing, or attempted escape, the child would suffer a more severe beating on the hand or back. If the punishment was so extreme as to endanger the child's health, he or she could ask for the punishment to be divided in two. Gerda was quite rightly horrified at seeing children suffer this sort of treatment. Mealtimes must have been torture for her.

This was the routine: after the meal, when all the dishes had been cleared away and the children were still sat at their tables, Sister Superior would serve the 'last dish'. She would slowly take the belt from her hip, hold it between her slim fingers, and say a few solemn words about the deep sorrow she felt about what she was about to do. She always pointed out the educational necessity of chastisement. Then she would call for a child – often a boy called Lubomir – and he would hold out his hand, swallowing his tears. Lubo never made a sound, so all the boys admired his bravery, though some of the watching children cried. A girl called Karolina was punished almost every day, but unlike Lubo, she would howl as she approached the dais. She was fifteen, one of the eldest there, and Gerda at just eleven and having no experience of such things couldn't understand why Karolina kept thieving despite the punishment that would inevitably follow.

Being a good, quiet and well-behaved girl, Gerda managed to evade such punishments at first, but then she was unfortunate enough to obtain two 'C' grades in her first term marks. Each 'C' was equivalent to a number three, which meant three strokes for each 'C'. Gerda had to walk up onto the dais, stretch out her hand, and take whatever the sadistic Sister decided to mete out. She was determined not to cry out. She wouldn't give the hated nun that satisfaction.

Recalling this event sixty years later, Gerda still felt the humiliation and the injustice. Nobody had ever punished her by inflicting pain before.

After a couple of months of this, Gerda was so desperate to escape she told Vera that they should try to return home. Vera replied that they didn't know where either of their parents was at this time, so it was pointless. Gerda said their mother had promised to write to tell them where she was – but Vera's response was that they hadn't seen any letters, and she thought it was perfectly okay in the orphanage anyway. If their parents had wanted them to stay with them, that's what would have happened – so clearly they didn't want them. Gerda couldn't understand how Vera could be so complacent. She threatened to run away by herself and say that Vera was responsible. Of course she didn't carry her plan through, and eventually a letter from their mother did arrive, but it was signed with a different name and gave no return address, so that was that. In the letter, she said she hoped the girls were getting used to their new surroundings and doing well in their studies. She looked forward to seeing them shortly. Gerda read the subtext as: 'My dear girls, the world has lost its senses, come to us so we can get over this madness or die together'. Vera, given her temperament, no doubt took the letter as an encouraging one – Gerda since spoke of how she was fully aware that her memories of this time and her sister's would be very different, given their different personalities.

The nuns were not uniformly malicious. Some could show genuine compassion. There was a woman called Milena in the orphanage who had some skills as a seamstress, so undertook odd sewing jobs. She suffered from epilepsy, and loved the warmth from the stoves that were dotted around the building. One drew her in particular. This was an oven in which the fire was intensely hot behind a heavy cast iron door. Sometimes she would open the oven door and lie down on the floor in front of it, not caring that the cinders would inevitably fall out.

One day she entered a classroom and sat down at the front of the class with the other students, though she certainly wasn't a member of the class, as she was far too old. She gazed out of the window where the tall cypresses were swaying in the wind, and must have become aware that an epilepsy attack was on the way. At such times she craved warmth. She left the classroom and lay stretched out on the floor in front of her favourite oven. The warmth was mesmerising, and she opened the door to watch the flames. Her head was too near the fire – which she didn't realise until her hair ignited, at which point she let out a shriek.

What happened next is not entirely clear. In Gerda's version of the tale, she was passing by and started shouting for help. She tried to drag Milena from the flames, but almost collapsed with the exertion while Milena merely grinned, apparently not minding the fact that she was on fire. Eventually some boys came along and dragged her to safety. In other accounts, nobody pulled her away – she realised what was happening and managed to save herself. What is clear is that the poor woman subsequently wandered around the classrooms with her singed hair, looking to Gerda like an apparition. The nuns never punished her, even though she had come close to burning down the orphanage.

Gerda was wretchedly unhappy in the orphanage itself, but found some solace at church. As soon as she sat on the wooden pew, she felt a sense of being apart from reality. Beyond the church walls lay loneliness and separation, but in the church she felt love and repose. She particularly loved the echoes and reverberations of the tall building. Sisters Anna and Žofia took the orphans to church every Sunday. Gerda found the wooden pews uncomfortable after the first half hour, but she loved the hymns and the sound of the organ. She didn't believe in God, but something in her chimed with the peace and spirituality of the environment, which was so different to the world outside. Pastor Derer's sermons were inspiring. He talked of the eventual victory of justice over oppression, and of the goodness of man. Gerda imagined seraphs hovering under the vaulted roof, and burst into song with gusto during the hymns. This was spoilt for her when a girl called Silvia who was sitting next to her nudged her in the ribs and complained she was out of tune. Gerda lost her confidence from then on and just mumbled the words. Occasionally, when alone, she would try to sing, but found she couldn't do it. This singing problem became a major emotional issue. She worried that her parents would not know her when they returned because of what had happened to her voice.

During the first few weeks at the orphanage, Gerda talked almost exclusively to Vera. She was too shy to make friends quickly, but eventually she formed a close bond with another girl, Šárka. Gerda couldn't understand what Šárka saw in her, but was grateful for the loving friendship she offered. For all that Šárka looked, in Gerda's eyes, like a blonde Virgin Mary, she was a worldly and experienced girl who could joke about what the nuns got up to with candles – and even demonstrate. All this was astonishing and new to Gerda.

There were other pleasures. Sister Julia sometimes took the girls out hiking, round the frozen lake in winter and into the vineyards in summer, and across the meadows at the edges of the forest in spring. Gerda let her imagination soar on these walks, though she always returned to the thought of one date: 30th July. This was the end of the school year and the time when her parents would come and collect her and Vera from this dismal place and take them on holiday as they'd promised.

Because of her general unhappiness Gerda couldn't even enjoy the school subjects she'd liked before. She sat as close to the window as she could and stared at the sky, blanking out whatever the teacher was saying. In music lessons, she hid behind the back of the girl in front of her so that the teacher would not realise she was miming rather than singing – she was afraid to sing as she knew the other girls would laugh at her voice. During one lesson, however, they didn't have to sing; they had a test to identify notes played to them. When it was Gerda's turn, she managed this easily, using the tonic sol-fa system. She achieved an 'A' grade, and reckons that was pretty much all the memorable education she received between the ages of seven and fourteen.

Most of the residents of Modra had no idea there were any Jewish families in the town, or hidden children in the orphanage and boarding school. A few, however, were aware of the fact, and some of these were rabid anti-Semites and informed the authorities that Pastor Derer was hiding Jews. One morning, when the girls were in class, a German officer walked into Pastor Derer's office and demanded a list of all the Jewish students who were boarding in the school. Pastor Derer denied there were any there. For whatever reason, the officer didn't want a confrontation at that point so he left, but the Pastor knew he would return. He asked his little son to run and find Sister Vera and tell her to find a way to get all the Jewish girls out of their classes, as quickly as possible. The Sister hurried from class to class, pretending she needed help, and picking out the few Jewish girls. She told the girls to run and hide in the orchard until she returned. If any strangers approached, they should go out through the back gate and hide in the vineyards that surrounded the school.

After a while the officer returned with a squadron of Gestapo and checked the names on the dormitories for any that sounded Jewish. He made his own list, and demanded the Pastor deliver these girls. The Pastor explained that these girls were no longer pupils at the school, but the office didn't believe him.

Meanwhile, in the orchard, the girls had dispersed in little groups. Gerda, Vera, and one of their friends walked for hours, not knowing what to do or what would happen next. They were hungry and thirsty and wanted their teacher to return to tell them it was safe as she'd promised. The sun went down and the three girls decided to return to the orphanage rather than the school. They left the orchard and entered the vineyard, crawling on the ground so that they wouldn't be seen. As they approached the road, they saw helmets and bayonets, so they crawled back into the vineyard and looked for a path that would enable them to bypass the road. They found one and walked along it and straight into a small square that felt as if the entire Third Reich had parked there. They tried to turn round, but a young soldier stopped them and asked where they were going. Gerda's friend was the first to find her voice, and said, 'Home.' The soldier smiled and said, 'Come with me.' He escorted them safely through the soldiers, who laughed and joked as to which girl was the prettiest. They reached the other side of the square, and the young soldier said, 'Run along, your mothers will be worried'. The girls needed no further encouragement. They ran.

Sister Žofia met them on the street. She said the nuns had been worried and had been trying to find the girls for hours. She grabbed Vera and her friend and pulled them along. Gerda was exhausted, terrified she would be left behind in the dark, but an old woman pointed the way for her, and she managed to catch up.

At last they arrived back and the nuns took them down to the cellar to hide them in case the Gestapo came back. In the event they were safe – their names had not been on the officer's list. Some of the other girls were not so lucky. A few managed to stay hidden in the orchard, but some had returned to the school. Six or seven of them were rounded up and taken away in lorries and were never seen again.

Gerda and Vera and their friend spent long days in the cellar. Sister Julia came down and taught Vera sewing, but Gerda was left in the corner, sick with loneliness, thinking nobody loved her any more, sad, aching, cold, neglected, her hair swarming with lice, and fungal infections growing between her fingers. She started having strange, hallucinogenic nightmares. Then one day she woke up and Sister Julia was sitting on the bed next to hers – she said she was glad to see Gerda's temperature was coming down at last. She brought Gerda a tray with a warm cup of milk, a soft-boiled egg and a slice of bread and butter. For one rare moment, Gerda was almost happy.

Summer came at last, and Ilona really did come to collect the girls, though she said, without going into details, that their father couldn't be there. To cheer them up, she told them about the Graf family, said she had become friendly with them, that they had a daughter, Hanka (Jana) who was only a little older than they were, so they would have a new friend – and possibly even a boyfriend, because Hanka had a brother.

When Gerda and Jana met, they hit it off immediately and soon became firm friends, a friendship that would last through decades. Pavel pulled Gerda's braids and teased her, which she took as a sign of him being keen on her. The families soon became very close and would go for frequent trips into the forests round the village. Gerda missed her grandmother and other relations, but couldn't nerve herself to ask her mother why they weren't visiting any more.

A week before the end of the holidays, a decision had still not been made as to whether the twins should return to the orphanage or not. There were rumours of an approaching uprising. People wondered if the partisans could overcome the regime, and if they were unsuccessful, what would happen to them. The adults were unable to hide their concern, so the children were very aware of the rising stress levels. In the event, the uprising did take place on the day before the twins' twelfth birthday. The streets were swarming with armed German soldiers so Ilona decided to get Gerda and Vera away quickly to a town north of Bratislava called Banská Bystrica, where they had some cousins. Gerda was relieved to be going anywhere other than the hated orphanage. They dressed in their best clothes, bought railway tickets and boarded the night train. The look of anxiety on her mother's face brought home to Gerda just how dangerous the situation was. Her mother was usually so good at hiding emotions.

They arrived at their destination at midnight, but could not leave the station because of the curfew. It soon became apparent that this was not a safe place to be as it was full of partisans, Hlinka Guards, Germans wielding truncheons and checking papers, people with bundles of possessions – everyone watching everyone else, all suspicious, all frightened. This was no good, so they took the first train back the next morning.

They arrived home and found their father there, packing hurriedly. He said he'd come back for some clothes and documents, but would not be able to return again. It was too risky. Ilona was exhausted. She knew her travel exemption from her workplace would soon be useless. There was nothing for it – the girls would have to return to the orphanage, however much Gerda hated the thought. Ilona would have to go into hiding herself under a false name. Their father sat the girls down and talked to them, reassuring them. The orphanage really was the safest place. The war would be over as soon as the Russians advanced. Gerda didn't argue. She had seen enough now to understand the dangers.

17

JANA JOINS GERDA

In 1944, Pastor Jurkovič finally succeeded in persuading Jana's family to hide her in the same Lutheran Orphanage in Modra that had taken Gerda and Vera the year before. It would mean a heartbreaking separation for them all, but Jana's safety was paramount. The Čermáks, from the old apartment block, had offered their dead daughter's birth and baptismal certificates to give Jana a new identity. This daughter would have been about a year older than Jana. The certificate wasn't needed in the event, as the orphanage was happy to take Jana in without any papers.

Pastor Dérer was unable to offer a place at the orphanage for Pavel. The reason given was that he was too old, but Jana thinks it might also have been that Jewish boys would normally have been circumcised, so could easily be identified in a way girls couldn't be. As it happens, neither Jirka nor Pavel had been circumcised due to Gustav's strongly held views against religious practices of any kind. Pastor Dérer didn't offer Jana a place as a boarder at the school, as the experience with the raid the previous year had shown this was too dangerous, so it would have to be the orphanage. When the girls from the boarding school had been deported, the pastor had gone to the authorities, utterly distraught, and offered himself in exchange for them, saying that they were to him like his own children. His offer was refused. The pastor's selfless act had put him in considerable danger, and had also risked his family. Many years later, Gerda and Vera Kaufmann, along with Jana, and those of the children who were still in touch with each other, put his name forward to be recognised as a 'righteous gentile'. He survived the war, but by the time he was awarded this honour of *Righteous Among the Nations*, he had sadly died, so the posthumous award was collected by his daughter. He is now commemorated at the *Yad Veshem Holocaust Memorial* in Jerusalem along with the hundreds of other non-Jews from all over Europe who took exceptional personal risks in their attempts to save persecuted Jews.

The decision was made, and Kamila and Jana took the train to Modra. When they arrived, Jana had as bad a first impression as Gerda had done the previous year, particularly when it came to the Sister in charge – Sister Žofia – who struck her as a very severe and forbidding woman. She kept her leather belt gripped in her hand at all the times, and Jana would soon see this in action at the dreaded mealtimes. When Kamila showed her Jana's school reports, Sister Žofia said she was very impressed. None of the other orphanage children had a report with so many 'ones'. She showed Jana where to put her things and which bed in the dormitory was to be hers, but that was that. It was an exact repeat of Gerda's introduction to orphanage life. There would be no gentleness, no kindness, and certainly none of the counselling that we take for granted for children in desperate situations these days. Jana said farewell to her mother, neither knowing if or when they would see each other again.

As far as Jana could tell, there were at least half a dozen other Jewish girls hidden in the orphanage, as well as one boy of about sixteen or seventeen who worked in the garden and did other odd jobs. An older Jewish woman – presumably the lady Gerda recalls as setting fire to her hair during an epileptic fit – was the resident seamstress. The orphanage couldn't obtain any rations for the Jewish children or the seamstress because they had no papers that could be safely shown to the authorities, but they accommodated them anyway and shared the food round as best they could. The Jewish children attended the church school with the other orphans and were treated exactly the same as everyone else. To have done any differently would have made them obviously 'different' and put them at grave risk of discovery. As well as Gerda and Vera Kaufmann, Jana also knew a few of the other orphanage girls, but it was impossible to tell who was Jewish and who was not as the subject was never mentioned. This was for safety reasons to ensure none of the children could let slip anything to the authorities. When the German soldiers came to check the dormitories and count the children, they managed to miss the extra ones, which suggests someone had done a clever job doctoring the paperwork.

Pastor Dérer was in overall charge, but the day to day running of the orphanage was down to the Lutheran nuns, who unfortunately had little idea of how to bring up children as Gerda had already discovered. The problem wasn't that they were prejudiced against the Jewish girls – in Jana's words they were 'equally nasty to all'. There were four nuns involved in the day to day running of the orphanage. Sister Žofia, who Jana considered a sadist, always went around looking for a reason to hit someone with her belt. She seemed to have a problem with names. For example, she called Alica 'Manca' and Jana was always 'Johana' – presumably a mixture of Jana and Hana, the name the Kaufmann sisters called her. The eldest of the nuns, Sister Paulina, was in charge of the kitchen. Sister Anna looked after the boys – she was the exception to the nastiness rule and was a lovely lady who was always ready to listen to any child. She was also in charge of all the pre-school children, as there were fewer boys than girls in the orphanage. Sister Julia was in charge of the girls and would have been okay except that she tended to have her favourites so the others would suffer from not being part of her set.

This wasn't a happy time for anyone. Jana had more resilience than Gerda, but still found the regime tough and uncompromising and was unable to take it all in her stride the way Vera did. She describes the place as being reminiscent of Lowood School in *Jane Eyre*: very old-fashioned and often unpleasant – but every single one of the hidden girls in the orphanage survived. Life might have been tough, but it was fundamentally safe.

Safety is one thing, comfort and compassion quite another. The nuns' lack of parenting skills made Jana particularly sorry for those children who had never experienced a loving home life. They would be beaten by Sister Žofia for almost any minor misdemeanour, even something as petty as a dirty fingernail. Unlike Gerda, Jana managed to avoid any beatings during her time at the orphanage. She did this by working hard to keep her run of high marks going, and by watching her step carefully at all other times. I think Gerda's problem in some ways was that she was too much of a dreamer. Jana was always more practical and down-to-earth, so more aware of how to keep out of trouble.

Discipline was strict and culture non-existent, which made a depressing change for a child like Jana who came from a home full of music, art and literature. The only music now was the singing of hymns in church every Sunday, where the orphanage children made up the choir. Unlike Gerda, Jana didn't find this remotely spiritually uplifting or musically satisfying. The only books available were the text books brought back from the school for doing homework. There were none kept at the orphanage for pure enjoyment: no novels or stories to enable the children to enter other worlds for brief periods in order to escape from the drudgery and unhappiness of their everyday existence. Luckily for Jana the curate discovered she liked reading and was happy to lend her reading matter, but this was the exception.

The washing facilities at the orphanage were very basic. The washroom contained about five washbasins which provided cold water only. There was one bath with a wood burning stove to heat the water. Jana was now introduced to the regime Gerda and Vera had been enduring for a whole year – one bath a week, two girls at time, with the water being changed only after every five baths, so ten children would have to share the same water. Gerda's memory was of no change of water, but I suspect given the numbers at the

135

orphanage, Jana's account has to be more accurate. Somehow Gerda and Jana managed to be the first pair in most times. Toilet paper in the lavatories was made from torn up newspaper. There were no blackout blinds or curtains in the dormitory windows, so the children had to go to bed in the dark. A bucket was provided for the use of anyone who needed the toilet in the night. The dormitory had one tiled heating stove which was lit about two hours before bedtime and then left to die out overnight. To light it, the girls carried a shovel full of embers from the kitchen up the stairs to the dormitory. Luckily there were never any mishaps. Every morning before going to school, two of the girls washed the staircase and then took the bucket of dirty water to the stream in the grounds to empty it and rinse out the washcloths. In winter, that meant breaking the ice first.

If a girl was unfortunate enough to get head lice, it was considered to be her own fault. She would be treated for the lice, and her hair cut short. If it happened to a younger girl, then it was the fault of the older one who was her 'carer', so as a punishment the older girl's hair would also be cropped.

Underwear, which comprised underpants and a slip, could only be changed once a week. Interestingly, Jana stopped menstruating when she arrived at the orphanage and didn't start again until she arrived in England at the end of the war. This might have solved the problem of sanitary protection, but also speaks volumes of the stresses of the situation. Sister Žofia made a vague attempt to explain the facts of life to the girls, particularly those like Vera Kauffman who did actually have periods while she was there, but as a nun, and a very embarrassed nun at that, she wasn't much use and the girls almost certainly knew more about it anyway.

Everyone was rationed at this time but the orphanage couldn't claim food for everyone, despite the creative paperwork. Jana didn't think the portions were very generous, unlike Gerda who thought there was too much food, but all of it inedible. The poor and monotonous diet comprised mostly haricot beans, potatoes and sauerkraut, thickened presumably with the mysterious 'grout' that Gerda hated so much. Meat was rare and usually in the form of a rather liquid goulash with potatoes. Lunch was sometimes just soup and a pudding, which would be something basic and stodgy like noodles sprinkled with poppy seeds and sugar. Everything would be eaten off the same metal dish, so you had to finish your first course as the sweet one would be shovelled on top of it. The only utensil was a spoon, to be used for both courses. The nuns, on the other hand, ate off china plates with knives and forks.

Breakfast was a chunk of bread washed down with linden tea. Sunday evenings were special, with bread and jam as a treat, but no butter or margarine. For Christmas dinner, the children tucked into a real pork sausage followed by white bread with poppy seeds, and milk to drink. Bread at all other times was of the dark rye variety. I tend to think of dark rye bread as a special treat and white bread as being cheap and nasty, but then I think of the story of *Heidi*, and the way she stored up the soft white bread rolls for her grandmother, not realising they'd go hard and stale, and I start to see the point.

The dishes were rinsed after meals and the water and accompanying waste food went to feed the pigs. The rinsed crockery would then be washed in fresh water with the addition of washing soda. The children's hands became red and raw with all this washing. One day Gerda slipped on the wet kitchen floor and smashed several plates. She thought she would be in terrible trouble, but for once it was agreed this was an accident and she was let off without punishment.

The children had somehow to find the energy from this nutritionally poor diet, which seems to have been high on carbs but low on everything else, to work hard at school as well as doing all the housework and kitchen chores. The nuns took on a purely supervisory role when it came to any sort of manual work. They presumably saw chores as useful training for the children, and certainly not something they should be doing themselves.

Shortly after arriving at the orphanage, Jana stopped hearing from her parents completely. They had promised to write regularly, so she didn't know what to do. If she wrote to someone to ask what had happened, she would betray where she was hidden. In the end, the need to know grew greater than her fear of discovery, so she wrote to the family's old friends the Čermáks. She told them where she was and asked for any information they could give her about her parents. Mrs Čermáková wrote back and assured her that her secret was safe, but she also had to give her the terrible news that her parents and Pavel had been deported. She didn't know much more, but she did send Jana some pocket money. This must have been agonising for Jana. People who were deported didn't come back. She had to somehow get her head round this and carry on as normal so as not to give anything away. This banking down of emotions – this hiding of everything that is important – it must have a fundamental and irrevocable effect on development, especially coming mid-teens as it did with Jana, and it must affect how easy or otherwise it is to express emotions with any sort of freedom in later life.

Each secondary school age girl in the orphanage was made responsible for a primary school child. This responsibility entailed making sure their hair was brushed, their bed made, their stockings darned, and any other little practical jobs were done efficiently. Jana was put in charge of an eight year old girl called Betka, who became quite devoted to her. She loved it when Jana read her stories, and would happily run errands for her. The nuns on the other hand showed no emotions towards their charges as a general rule. They saw their responsibilities as teaching the Bible and caring for the children's basic physical wellbeing. Anything more would be considered inappropriate. The only affection the children could receive was therefore from each other. The devotion of Betka to Jana showed a need for personal attachment which the little girl couldn't get from those who were supposed to be caring for her. Some of the other girls, like Gerda and

Šárka, developed close physical relationships with each other, as was bound to happen in this sort of situation.

There were also some very young pre-school children who were looked after by a girl of about fifteen who had already left school. Occasionally this girl was allowed a Sunday off to go to church followed by a free afternoon. On these days, one of the other girls took over the infants' care, despite having no training or instruction of any kind. When it was Jana's turn, she enjoyed doing it but was exhausted by the end of the day.

The secondary age girls attended lessons in the boarding school, which was also attended by day children from the town of Modra, while the primary age children and secondary boys went to the local state schools. Lessons in the Lutheran boarding school began at eight in the morning and continued until one or two in the afternoon, with a break for a substantial 'elevenses' at ten o'clock. The boarders and orphanage girls would usually be given some leftovers from whatever the boarders had eaten at the previous evening meal, which might be something like pasta or burgers. That sounds extraordinarily modern, but of course meat patties have been around forever and pasta for centuries.

All the teachers at this school were referred to as 'Aunties'. The headmistress was 'Aunty' Masha. There was also an Aunty Olga, Aunty Irena and Aunty Viera, who was the daughter of the minister. The children referred to these three amongst themselves as Chekhov's *Three Sisters*.

Aunty Masha called Jana into her office one day. She knew her background and presumably with the best intentions tried to persuade her that her parents hadn't been deported; they must have disappeared in order to go into hiding. Jana wasn't convinced as she was sure Mrs Čermáková's information was reliable. It was still a kind gesture, if misguided.

The boarding school had been housed in decent buildings, so these were inevitably requisitioned by the army and the school had to move into the orphanage. This meant the mid-morning break food was no longer pasta and burgers

– it was a piece of dry bread. The day pupils from the town brought their own food and couldn't believe how badly the others were fed. On one occasion one of the day girls found an apple in her desk – nobody claimed it so the other girls decided it would be a kind gesture to give it to Jana, as she was an orphanage child. Jana thanked them for their generosity, but pretended she didn't like apples. Of course she loved apples really, but she didn't want to be in receipt of charity – a decision which in hindsight strikes her as being very silly.

Jana and another girl were sometimes sent to help the lady who cleaned the church before the Sunday service. One Saturday after they'd done their cleaning duties, the lady in charge of them had failed to check that all was well before she left. When the children marched into church on Sunday morning, one can imagine the muffled giggles when they noticed the broom had been left against the altar and there was a duster draped over the altar rail – a purely accidental illustration of cleanliness being next to godliness. The girls were in disgrace. How they avoided a beating is a mystery.

The monotonous daily routine at the orphanage meant you got up, went to school, worked all day, came back to the orphanage to do your homework, and in filled in any remaining time with domestic chores: cleaning, peeling potatoes, washing up, and scrubbing floors. Sunday morning was church, so the only semblance of leisure time allowed was Sunday evenings, when you might manage a quiet game of ludo or something equally innocuous and dull with your friends. Such activities were not permitted at any other time. The nuns did not approve of leisure. If a child wasn't engaged in doing their homework, a chore could easily be found to keep them gainfully occupied and no doubt free from whatever temptations the nuns chose to imagine. It must have felt as if these tedious routines were going to continue forever.

As well as a conspicuous lack of books in the orphanage, there was also a lack of toys and only a very scant collection of board games. I've seen a photograph taken one Christmas of all the orphanage children and the four nuns in front of the Christmas tree. A glum little boy has been posed on a rocking horse, which I suspect was brought in especially for the photo. Three of the four nuns pictured have signed the back of the photograph – Sister Žofia, Sister Paulina and Sister Julia. I'm sure the nuns were doing their best in difficult circumstances, but I've never seen such a miserable set of people gathered round a tree. It was probably at this Christmas that a textile merchant kindly donated some bales of cloth which were made into new dresses for all the girls in the orphanage – red checked for the younger ones and blue checks for the older ones. The boys had new winter trousers. When the Kaufmann twins and Jana eventually left the orphanage, they were allowed to take the dresses with them, so that when they went to school later in Bratislava dressed in their matching gingham finery, people thought they were triplets.

Sister Paulina's brother sometimes came to help out at the orphanage – mainly with the boys, also simply so that there would be another male around the place to safeguard the girls. The only other man was the curate. Sister Paulina's brother only lasted a week or two. Jana suspects he was getting too friendly with the older girls. He'd apparently taken to examining their hands and explaining to them how to care for their fingernails.

Jana was a teenager by this time, so naturally was going to notice and get noticed by the boys. She grew particularly friendly with a boy called Vlado Makyš who was a year or so older than she was. He made his affections clear by sharing his sweet ration with her. When he turned fifteen, he had to leave to become an apprentice, so the two youngsters arranged secretly to meet late after lights out on the staircase that connected the girls' and boys' houses to say goodbye. This was Jana's first kiss. In Jana's words, the two of them would have been 'skinned alive' if any of the

141

nuns had caught them at it, but luckily they weren't discovered.

Jana never saw Vlado again.

18

PAVEL'S STORY

It is only recently that Pavel has felt able to tell the story of what happened to him during this time. This has been thanks to the support of a memoir writing group at his home in New Jersey, and also the unexpected discovery of a fellow resident who had been through similar experiences. Only those who lived through the same traumas could really know what it was like. This chapter is based entirely on Pavel's testimony, given with his blessing for the purposes of this book.

Sometime in the autumn of 1944, after Jana had been safely hidden in the orphanage, two Nazis arrived unexpectedly at midday to pick the family up. They asked where Jana was, and Gustav told them she was at school in a nearby village. He also said that Kamila was not Jewish. She didn't look it, so he might have got away with the lie, but it angered the Nazis who said they had records proving she was Jewish. They struck Gustav and he fell to the ground. The family was told to pack their best clothes and whatever food they had and to wait in the house. They did as they were told. They had no choice.

    While they were waiting in the kitchen, Kamila urged Pavel to escape through the window. She gave him an address of some people who she hoped could safely hide him until the end of the War. He was unconvinced. He thought he would be safer with the peasants who had let them sleep in the haystack. He said if the Nazis started shooting at him, he

143

would run in zigzags so that they would miss him. Gustav said no, this was far too dangerous. Kamila thought he should still try; he should run – and it struck Pavel that this was the first time he had ever heard his parents arguing with each other. He had to make up his own mind quickly. Although his instinct was to do what his mother was advising, to run and get out of there at any cost – he decided to follow his father's advice instead, so he stayed put.

The Nazis returned, put the family into a car and drove them to the neighbouring village of Lamač to pick up the Ehrensteins. The Ehrenstein's adult son had left illegally some time before. They also tried to pick up the Kaufmanns, along with their daughters, Gerda and Vera, but the girls were already in hiding in the orphanage so couldn't be found.

The family was driven to the central office in Bratislava and Gustav was led off to be interrogated. The Nazis suspected Jana might have been placed in the orphanage, so they went and searched the place, but they couldn't find any sign of her.

Two days later the family were taken to Sered distribution camp where they remained for a week. On one particular day, Pavel was walking from one section to another when a fat Nazi guard started shouting angrily at him, not liking his attitude. The guard was shaking so much with fury that his ammunition fell on the ground. When he bent down to pick it up, Pavel slipped away into the crowd, crouching down so he couldn't be seen.

Mr. Ehrenstein's name was called on the loud speaker. He and the camp commandant were apparently old acquaintances from the philatelic circle. It's possible he was released thanks to this friendship, but he was never heard of again, even after the war, so it's impossible now to know exactly what happened to him.

The people in the camp were separated into two groups: men in one, women and children in the other. As a sixteen year old, Pavel would still have been considered a child, but he thought he would have a better chance of survival as an adult so told those in charge that he was eighteen. They believed him, and put him with his father amongst the other men.

They were all forced into a crowded cattle car. The train moved north slowly and some of the men panicked, thinking they must be heading for the extermination camp at Auschwitz. Many wanted to jump out of the train, and this time Gustav urged Pavel to go with them, but he refused. The cattle car door could only be opened from the outside, so one man broke the small window above the door in the hope that someone with long arms would be able to reach the outside door handle through the broken window, but just at that moment the train stopped. Guards were walking up and down outside, inspecting the cars. Inevitably, they noticed the broken window. They shouted, "Who did it?" At first there was no response, so the guards said they would kill everyone unless someone confessed, in which case they said they would only kill every tenth person. One brave man – not the one who had broken the window – raised his hand. The guards took him away. He was a hero, without any doubt.

The guards had been bluffing, however. They didn't come back and kill every tenth man. Instead, they moved everyone to another locked cattle car. This one couldn't be opened from the outside without a key. The train turned left towards the West. They were not going to Auschwitz after all.

The cattle car was so crowded that they had to take it in turns to sit on the floor. Most had to stand. One man died and it took almost a day to remove his body. The cattle cars obviously had no toilets. The men were told they could relieve their bowels between cars when the train stopped. They had to say: *Ich will sheissen* (I have to shit). Pavel's German was not good, and he said: *Ich will shiessen* (I will shoot you). The guard was at first angry, but then he started to laugh. He was Hungarian, and Hungarians have a good sense of humour, so Pavel was very lucky. The guard taught him how to say it correctly for the next time.

145

The journey took four days, continuing past Gustav's birthplace and on to Sachsenhausen, a suburb north of Berlin. Everything they had packed and brought with them was confiscated at this point. Gustav and Pavel had managed to eat a tin of sardines before their belongings were taken away. They left the train and were told they were going to march to Oranienburg, a suburb West of Berlin. Those that could not march would go by truck. Gustav was not a strong walker, so he boarded the truck. Pavel was very concerned, thinking they might kill everyone in the truck.

During the march he saw one person at the back of the line who couldn't keep up. The guards kept hitting the back of his knees with the butts of their rifles and he kept collapsing. Pavel tried to help him and dragged him along to speed up his progress. It never occurred to him that this would put him in danger. Soon the guards were hitting the back of his knees too, but another walker joined him and they managed to drag along the weak man along between them so that he could keep up.

Pavel and Gustav were reunited in Oranienburg inside a huge hangar, part of which had been bombed. There were already other inmates in Oranienburg, mostly political prisoners. While they were there, Gustav taught Pavel the second and third verses of the Czech national anthem. When sung, the anthem generally only used the first verse, which Pavel already knew. Gustav also told Pavel where the family's grand piano and other items they had owned had been stored.

Pavel soon realised that if anyone didn't follow orders to the letter or quickly enough, the Nazis would make sure they were beaten. They didn't do this themselves, but would enlist the services of any prisoners they knew to be anti-Semitic, and watch while they carried out the punishment.

A week later they marched or were taken in trucks back to Sachsenhausen. Once there, Pavel saw some prisoners who were being made to push the spokes of a huge horizontal wheel. The guards forced them to go faster and faster, until they collapsed, at which point they were beaten to death.

The men were separated again, this time by age, young from old. Pavel was frightened that he might not see his father again and held his hand very firmly so that he wouldn't be able to join the group of older men. A guard saw what he was doing and struck Pavel so hard on his right ear that he fell. The blow caused him to suffer vertigo attacks subsequently. When the guards had finished dividing the groups and were looking the other way, some from the old group crossed over to join the younger men. Pavel was desperate for Gustav to do the same, but he again refused. Pavel wondered if he wanted to die because he felt responsible for Jirka's fate. He had cancelled several illegal crossings from Bohemia and Moravia to Slovakia, each time saying it was too dangerous even though it was accepted that Slovakia had been the safer country at the time. There had been various ways to cross the border: a guide might lead you through the forest, you might go in a locomotive as the fireman, or you could possibly find some other way. At one point Pavel had wanted to arrange an illegal crossing himself, without the knowledge of his parents. .

Pavel looked for Gustav later and found him by going across to his block. This was a dangerous thing to do, and at first he didn't recognizing his father because his trademark beard had been shaved off. This was the last time Pavel would speak to him. He assumed he would most likely die like the men he'd seen pushing the spokes of the wheel.

The elder men were left at Sachsenhausen and the younger men taken by train to Buchenwald, less than a day's uneventful trip away.

In the meantime, Kamila had been taken from Sered to Ravensbrück, where she may also have wanted to die as she would have assumed – incorrectly – that none of her children were going to survive. Mrs Ehrenstein was with her, and told Máňa after the war that they had separated the women between old and young. Kamila had told them her

147

real age, but Mrs Ehrenstein had lied. She survived as a result, but Kamila died.

Pavel managed to survive Buchenwald, but Gustav died in Sachsenhausen. Jana knew none of this at the time. As far as she was aware, she was now entirely alone.

19

OTTO AND MÁŇA ON THE ROAD

At this point I'm going to backtrack a little to pick up Máňa's story. She will reappear in the main narrative shortly, so I thought I'd give a brief account of how she and her husband Otto survived the war years. This information comes from Otto's diary entries, which Jana later translated.

Otto and Máňa had decided to leave Slovakia shortly after their marriage in 1939. Máňa had been able to obtain a visa for France, so made her way directly to Paris. Otto could only get a visa for Italy, so he went there first, claiming he needed to travel for singing lessons with his former teacher, Fernando Carpi, who was then living Milan. Once he was in Italy, he was able to get a permit to enter France. He joined Máňa in Paris and they soon became part of the Czech artistic group there. This was an extraordinary collection of musicians, writers and painters, which included the eminent pianist Rudolf Firkušný, who had arrived in Paris in 1939 from Moravia. He had studied with the greats – Afred Cortot and Artur Schnabel – and was already an outstanding performer. Also amongst their number was the composer Bohuslav Martinů, who wrote compositions specifically for Firkušný to play as a result of their time together in Paris. Martinů had been in Paris since 1923, having received a scholarship to go there to study. In 1937 he became acquainted with the composer and conductor Vítězslava Kaprálová. Their friendship grew, and at one point they planned to move together as a couple to America, despite the fact that Martinů was still married to French seamstress Charlotte Quennehen. By autumn 1939, however, Kaprálová had fallen for another of their set, the writer and journalist Jiři Mucha. The two of them married, but Kaprálová sadly died of tuberculosis at the age of twenty-five just two months after her wedding. Another member of the artistic community was the painter Rudolf Kundera. A rumour was started by Mucha that Máňa had developed an excessive fondness for this Francophile colourist – a friend of the writer Claude Mauriac and poet Paul Valéry – but when Otto asked Máňa if this were true, she replied, 'Don't be so silly,' so we'll never know. Kundera died in 2005, still living in France, at the age of ninety-three.

Paris might have been culturally rich, but financially, Máňa and Otto were having dire problems and struggled to make any money. In his 1940 diary, Otto mentions that one day their total cash was down to the precarious amount of 20,60F. They had to live on handouts from various organisations plus any money Otto could make from the small number of paid musical engagements that were available. These were not well paid. He made just 5,20F for each rehearsal of a show called *Velbloud*, which I'm assuming was the play *Velbloud uchem jehly* (Camel through the eye of a needle), written by František Langer in 1923. These fees, however small, helped to keep them going. The first night of *Velbloud* was 6th April, 1940. Other engagements at this time included concerts with Rudolf Firkušný and Vítězslava Kaprálová. One of these was a Štepháník memorial concert at which Otto sang Dvořák's *Biblical Songs* accompanied by Kaprálová on the church organ.

Otto's diary entry for 9th February 1940 reads: 'Máňa operation'. No illness is mentioned, but Jana has always assumed this was for an abortion. The doctor's fee was 50F.

By the end of the first week of June 1940, the German army were nearing Paris. The city was no longer safe, and things could only get worse, so the little artistic community was forced to break up. Otto and Máňa decided their best move would be to head south. They left Paris on the 10th of June, hitching a ride in a truck towards Poitiers, a medieval town about half way down France towards the west coast. That night was spent in the open by the roadside. When they arrived the following day at Poitiers, they had difficulties finding accommodation due to the flood of refugees pouring in day and night. On the 15th, they slept at a farm where they left behind two suitcases. I don't know if they hoped to pick them up later, but presumably they had realised they would travel far more quickly and easily without too much luggage. They continued by truck, due south to Agen. On the 17th they left for Lourdes, not far from the foothills of the Pyrenees, where they slept in a hotel cellar. The next day they went on by truck south-east to Arreau, spending the night nearby in Cadéac. They left Arreau by another truck, then back-tracked and caught a bus to Tarbes, near Lourdes, presumably because this had a railway station. From here, they managed to catch the last train to Bayonne, near Biarritz and the coast.

Road and rail travel over, now it was time to continue by sea. They embarked on the cargo ship *Divona*, heading for Casablanca. I've looked her up – the *Divona* was a general cargo ship that had been built in 1918 by McMillan & Son in Dumbarton and was destined to be scuttled near Bizerte, Tunisia, in 1946, only a couple of years after Otto and Máňa sailed in her. The crossing was horrendously stormy. Everyone except for Otto was sick. For the next four nights, the passengers had to sleep on deck. When they finally arrived off the coast of Morocco, the ship was refused permission to dock, so the refugees were transferred to another ship – the hospital ship *Canada*. More refugees arrived on board, but this ship was going nowhere. Everyone was eventually transferred to yet another ship, and then taken ashore to a holding camp. The Czechs and Poles were told they would have to leave Morocco, which was fair enough, as nobody particularly wanted to stay, but they didn't know how or where they could go. Food in the camp was poor and the water almost undrinkable due to being over-chlorinated – but at least it didn't poison them..

The Czech Consulate was of no help, but assistance came from the unlikely quarter of the owners of the shoe company *Baťa*. This company had been founded by Tomáš Baťa back in 1894, and soon became very successful. During the First World War, the company had cut shoe prices by half and become even more profitable as a result, eventually setting up factories worldwide. After Tomáš died, his son and grandson continued the business. During the Second World War, they tried to make sure their Jewish workers inside Czechoslovakia were posted elsewhere. It's perhaps less well known that they were philanthropists who also helped refugees who were nothing to do with the shoe business, but it was with their help that Otto and Máňa were able to move on.

They managed to obtain both English and Canadian visas as well as an American transit visa, all of which were valid until the 30th September, so they had high hopes despite being shunted around – this time to another camp where they had to sleep on the floor. Time passed very slowly as they waited an interminable time to be assigned a place on a ship to the USA or Canada. Just as they thought they might be able to leave, their hopes were dashed again when they were told they had to stay in Morocco. Their visas were now useless, but they managed to obtain alternate ones for Portugal, and finally boarded a ship, the *Amour de Travail*. The first night was a repeat of their original voyage, with everyone being sick. They spent several days and nights on this ship with no shelter and very little food or drink. Eventually the ship turned round and sailed back to Casablanca. After docking, they were offered a place on a different ship to Lisbon, and were asked to give a ring as a deposit. In desperation, they agreed. On the 14th September, they finally embarked on the *Mar Azul*, in the company of other Czechs including the violinist Jan Boleslav Šedivka. This ship, for a change, didn't turn back, but made it all the way to Lisbon.

On arrival, they were housed in the jail at São Bruno de Caxias Fort, a building that has been recently restored, but which back in 1940 was probably not much changed from when it was originally built in 1647. Máňa and Otto had semi-celebrity status due to Otto's fame as a singer, so their stories appeared in the local press. They hoped they'd be able to leave soon for the States, and so started saying goodbye to their friends. These included Erna and Míla Stein, who were living in Lisbon as Erna was in the consular service. It was Míla who all those years later would impress me with her mushroom identification skills, but in all the years I knew her, I only thought of her as an 'old Czech friend' who gave my mother off-cuts of fabric to make into dresses for me. I had no idea of her history or that she had known my uncle and aunt in when they were in Lisbon.

On the 6th of October, Máňa and Otto set sail for Gibraltar, arriving just in time for it to be bombed. This was to be the pattern for the next few stages of their journey. On 18th October, they left Gibralter on the *SS Reina del Pacifico*. This was a famous ship. Built in 1931 for the Pacific Steam Navigation Company, she held the record of twenty-five days for the trip from Liverpool to Valparaiso, Chile, via the Panama canal. Throughout the duration of the Second World War she was used as a troopship. The voyage from Gibraltar to Liverpool was fairly hair-raising one, travelling in convoy and dodging U-boats, but everyone survived. The ship itself was finally scrapped in Wales in 1958.

Máňa and Otto landed in Liverpool on 25th October just in time for an air-raid. The next day they caught a train to London, arriving in time for yet another air-raid. They spent the night in a shelter and the next day made their way to the refugee centre. After sleeping in fields, on open ships and in a Portuguese jail, at last, on 31st October, they were provided with decent accommodation in London's East End. Now that they were settled at last, they could make contact with other friends, including an uncle of Otto's – also, confusingly, called Otto Kraus – who was living in London at this time with his French wife. Otto tried to enlist at this point, but was refused as he was considered unfit due to heart problems. He and Máňa eventually became fed up with trooping down to the shelter every night during air raids, so stopped going all together, despite the house next to them being bombed.

Once established in London, Máňa managed to obtain a job with the Czechoslovak Government in Exile, and later on at the Czechoslovak Embassy and the foreign section of the BBC. Otto was invited to give occasional recitals in factories, where he was usually accompanied by Walter Susskind. They performed mostly folk songs, rather than grand opera. He also became the chief baritone of the Carl Rosa Opera Company, often being conducted by the great Vilém Tauský. One of the Carl Rosa's leading sopranos was Joan Hammond, who after she retired to her home in Australia, would send aspiring singers all the way from there to study with Otto.

They moved into a flat just behind Marble Arch which they shared at first with the Muchas, who had also made it to London. When the Muchas eventually moved back to Prague after the war, Máňa and Otto settled in a flat in Chepstow Court, Notting Hill, which is where we will rejoin them in a few chapters' time.

Throughout all their travelling, Máňa was in the same position as both Pavel and Jana, having no idea of who, if anyone had survived from their family, and fearing the worst all the time, but when the war finally ended, it would be Máňa who would be in a position to do something about it.

20

A SACK OF APPLES

In the last winter before the end of the war, five young men appeared at the orphanage. It was rumoured that they had come from Yugoslavia. They were clearly not orphans. All were wearing good clothes and looked at least eighteen. The girls believed they were partisans escaping the Gestapo, or maybe trying to initiate an uprising. One of them, Peter, showed an interest in Gerda. He didn't tease her like Pavel had – instead, he flattered her and was extremely polite. He took her skating on the frozen lake. They didn't have ice skates as such, but wearing thick soled shoes, they managed to slide well enough along the paths on the lake made by the villagers. Gerda would slide first, with Peter immediately behind her, catching up and giving her a hug. He laughed a lot, was always content and self-assured. Gerda began seeing the lake as enchanted, and for the first time in her life started to enjoy skating. She tried to get Vera to go with her, but Vera would rarely co-operate, and Gerda wondered if she was jealous of her friendships with both Peter and Jana. Winter eventually drew to an end and the ice began to melt.

Easter arrived at last and all the orphanage children trooped into church for the Good Friday service. In a couple of days' time, on Easter Sunday, Jana was due to be confirmed. She was fully rehearsed and ready to go, though not exactly keen as she shared her father's atheism and always would. The children left the church and returned to the orphanage. They went to bed as normal, accompanied by the rumble of distant fighting. The very next day, the Soviet army marched in and the church exploded. Jana was 'saved' in the nick of time from being confirmed, and everything changed for her yet again.

During the early months of 1945, the Soviet front had been drawing ever closer. The army had invaded Silesia and Pomerania in February, and by March they were heading towards their final destination of Berlin, going via Vienna, which was just a stones' throw from Bratislava. They crossed the border from Hungary to Austria on March 30th. On 2nd April they approached Vienna from the south. They surrounded, besieged and attacked the city. Two days later, on 4th April, it was neighbouring Bratislava's turn.

The nuns and the older girls had taken to sleeping in the attic with a large wardrobe pushed against the door to hide the entrance, but when the bombardment began, it wasn't safe to be upstairs any more. Most of Good Friday was spent in church with the nuns no doubt putting all their faith in God, though I have my doubts as to whether the hymn-singing and general piety was able to drown out the fear. By Saturday there was open fighting in the street, with no chance of going to church unless you had a death wish and particularly wanted to be shot. The nuns and children huddled together in the cellars. They slept on sacks of potatoes, which were hideously uncomfortable, even with the assistance of a blanket. On Sunday morning – the day of Jana's proposed confirmation – they couldn't have gone back to church even if they'd wanted to as it had been reduced to a heap of rubble. The Germans had been keeping arms in the crypt and the Soviets had torched the building, which is how it came to explode.

The army's advance had been preceded by terrifying rumours of rape and pillage. The first wave of soldiers looked as if they were going to live up to expectations, so all the women and girls stayed off the streets and kept away from the usually drunk soldiers, who allegedly would drink anything, including eau de cologne. Many wore strings of watches on their arms and seemed accountable to nobody.

There was just one victim, however, that they knew – a woman, connected with the orphanage, who lived in a private house nearby. She was shot, either defending her honour or her property. Gerda couldn't understand any of it. These soldiers were supposed to be here to liberate them from the Germans, yet they robbing and killing and raping. The second wave of Russians was thankfully far more civilised and disciplined.

The nuns and children awaited the inevitable discovery. Two Soviet soldiers soon came upon them, hidden in the cellar. The soldiers were puzzled, not certain of what they'd stumbled across. They asked if this was a school, or if not, what? The curate spoke some Russian and was able to explain to the soldiers that no, this wasn't a school – these were children and nuns from the orphanage. The soldiers took no immediate action. They left, presumably to obtain further orders, and the children stayed put as it wasn't safe to do anything else. They must have been wondering what would happen next, and imagining the worst.

The soldiers returned later that evening with two sacks of apples for everyone. After all the rumours of their behaviour, this was the last thing anyone had expected. The apples may well have been purloined from a neighbouring farm, but nobody was going to ask where they'd come from or put in an official complaint. The soldiers chatted, and said they had not seen their families since they started fighting and knew nothing of their fate. Everyone started to relax a bit and feel maybe they really had been liberated.

Within a few days, the Soviet Army had decided to make Modra their headquarters, so the children and nuns were told they would have to leave. I'm sure they were happy enough to comply. Within days they had decamped to the nearby village of Králová, where they were accommodated in the village school. They made the journey mostly on foot, carrying what they could on their backs. What couldn't be carried was loaded into cart pulled by a horse that was too old to be considered useful by the army.

The school that was used to accommodate them consisted of just two large rooms. One was turned into the boys' dormitory, and the other the girls'. The nuns slept on a curtained stage in the girls' room. This was living at its most basic. Sleeping had to be two to a bed because of the limited space, and they were so tightly packed the children had to crawl over each other to get to their own beds. The conditions might have been primitive, but everyone knew the war was coming to the end, so they were determined to cope. Some normal activities could even start up again, like the daily walk to the bakery to collect the freshly baked loaves.

There had always been occasional outbreaks of scabies amongst the orphanage children. The treatment was to be scrubbed all over with a hard floor brush. These infections became particularly widespread now due to the overcrowding. Luckily there were no worse epidemics.

The school buildings had no kitchen as such, but meals still had to be cooked. Although it was spring time, it wasn't yet warm – I'm writing this chapter in an unseasonably cold late March as it happens, with a blizzard going on outside, so I can imagine what this must have been like. All the cooking had to be done outdoors in huge cauldron-like pots over fires. Everyone, children and nuns alike, had to sit on the steps or on the ground in the school yard to eat their meals. At least the food was hot and nobody was bombing them; no churches were exploding and no one was fighting in the streets any more.

Gerda, Vera and Jana often talked amongst themselves about their parents and what might have happened to them. Gerda in particular dreamed of happy reunions. I suspect Vera and Jana were less optimistic. They never talked to the nuns about any of this, and the nuns never volunteered any information that wasn't related to the daily routine, so they carried on, day by day, with nobody knowing when or how things might change.

One day the girls were returning from the bakery with arms full of warm loaves when they saw an enthusiastic crowd gathered outside the school. It was obvious something

158

happy was taking place. As they came nearer, they recognised two of the people in the crowd. Gerda cried out, 'It's Mama and Papa!' dropped the loaves and rushed forwards. Hugo and Ilona were thin, shabbily dressed, but they were there, they had really come as they had promised. Ilona and Gerda openly wept; Vera and Hugo embraced wordlessly. Jana stood by, watching. She must have been happy for her friends, but heartbroken at the same time, as she would have been sure she wasn't ever going to have the same sort of happy reunion. The ever-optimistic Gerda went up to her and told her that her own parents and brothers would return soon as well, and she fully expected her grandmother to be nearby. Hugo became serious at this point and explained to Gerda that they didn't know what had happened to grandmother, and would have to go to Bratislava to find out. He and his wife were lucky to have got to Modra without being shot, as they hadn't realised the Russians had barred civilians from entering the town.

Gerda was desperate to leave with them at once, but her father explained this was simply not possible. She would have to be patient and wait a few more weeks. The 'normal life' that she wanted to resume could not happen. It was impossible. This was not 1939 any more. It was painful to have to say goodbye yet again, but it had to be done. Hugo and Ilona needed to find the family somewhere to live, to find out what had happened to their friends and relations, to find whatever of their possessions still remained. Eventually Gerda understood she had to accept this situation and stay with the nuns for just a little while longer.

The school teachers from Modra had been evacuated to various farms nearby, but it wasn't possible for lessons to continue as the school classrooms had both been turned into dormitories, meaning there was nowhere for lessons to take place.

One of the school teachers was living with her sister and her sister's young baby in the village. This teacher asked for an orphanage girl to come and live with them and help with looking after the baby. Jana volunteered immediately – anything to leave the drudgery of the orphanage with its dirt and chores and overcrowding and huge cauldrons of watery cabbage. The teacher and her sister were happy with the arrangement, so Jana managed to spend the last month of the war living in a little farmhouse looking after a baby. She loved it. This was the first time in ages she had felt as if she were being treated as a real human being. She became a normal person, caring for an infant and taking it out in the pram for walks. This happiness was, of course, tempered by the unknowing. There had still been no news of her family, and she didn't share Gerda's optimism that everything would be all right. She was frightened for her parents, having received that letter from Mrs Čermáková. She didn't know what had happened to Pavel either, and she didn't even know if Otto and Máňa had escaped. Like many others, she took to sitting by the radio as much as she could in the hope of hearing some news. There were regular hour long broadcasts every day with messages from people who were looking for survivors. She listened and listened, but there was never any mention of her parents. They would have known she'd been in the orphanage at Modra, but wouldn't have known about the orphanage moving to Králová, so she listened and hoped and listened some more in case there was news of them and they were trying to find her – but there was nothing.

This is something that still haunts her today: this listening for news, for a name, anything – all the time hoping, never knowing, always fearing the worst. Soon she would know for certain.

21

REDISCOVERY

No amount of optimism could hide the fact that Jana really was an orphan now rather than a hidden child with parents still living who would eventually return to collect her. It was suggested therefore that she should move to a different orphanage which had access to a grammar school as she was clearly academically more suited to that sort of education than the one she had been receiving. Jana later found out from one of Sir Martin Gilbert's books that this other orphanage also had a pastor who had been saving Jewish children. The orphanage was willing to take her, but Hugo and Ilona Kaufmann said no – she should could come and live with them as a third daughter. From her point of view this was infinitely preferable as she'd be with friends and in a proper family rather than all alone in another hated institution. The arrangements were agreed, so she went back to Bratislava to live with them in May 1945 in what would be the next step in a return to normal life.

The Kaufmanns had found a temporary flat thanks to Ilona's old employer who had given her a job again. This was in Eastern Bratislava, in Tehelne Pole, in a fairly utilitarian workers' block of flats. It was an unsettling and strange time. Many people would let off celebratory fireworks at night, which could be terrifying and joyful in equal measure. Shops were very poorly supplied with food. The only things that seemed to be plentiful were dried plums and popcorn. Some days they ate little else, apart from some decaying potatoes, but one day Hugo returned from town with a packet of cocoa powder. Ilona mixed it with milk powder and sweetener and made them all cups of delicious hot cocoa – a rare feast. As things improved, Ilona was able to get hold of white flour. She would take a kilo of flour to a nearby bakery early in the morning and collect the bread rolls at midday. There were also parcels sent from relatives in the US. These included disgusting fish oil pills that Hugo insisted the girls take every day, but also very much more welcome assorted chocolates. Hugo kept the chocolates locked away, as he knew Ilona would give in to nagging and let the girls have them all at once. He distributed them daily after dinner, so that the girls always had a treat to look forward to and could bear the oily pill for the sake of the chocolate.

Food supplies improved slowly but steadily. Towards the end of the year, they were eating meat, butter, and cheese, and Hugo was working again, having been able to re-establish his stamp catalogue publishing.

The girls had returned to school. This was a bit odd as it was located in a converted department store, the original school buildings having been used as an army hospital, but they didn't stay there long as school finished at the end of June for the summer holidays. Jana worked hard, as was her custom, but Gerda was having difficulties, and was suffering from frequent fevers and panic attacks. She felt too tall and clumsy, and still worried about not being able to sing. She felt everyone must be finding her utterly repulsive. Today we would probably say she was suffering from post traumatic stress syndrome. I'm sure her parents understood her problems, but they would not have been equipped to do much to solve them other than to try to keep everything as normal, safe and loving as possible.

At the school, German tuition was quickly dropped from the curriculum and replaced with Russian, but there were no Russian teachers. The German teacher was told 'You are the language teacher; so teach Russian.' The poor teacher tried to keep one lesson ahead of her pupils, but it was difficult for her as the languages were so different, with not even an alphabet in common. Thanks to Jana's earlier studies from the *Teach Yourself Russian* book she knew more than the teacher and would often correct her, which was probably not the best way to make herself popular.

Ilona Kaufmann had been a champion swimmer as a young woman. Jana had been able to swim from an early age thanks to going swimming with her mother even before she could walk, but when Ilona took her swimming and saw her lack of style, she took it upon herself to improve her technique. Jana doesn't think she was the best of swimming pupils. I've seen my mother swimming on holidays, and think she has a point. She stays afloat well enough and makes stately progress in the intended direction, using that very ladylike style of breaststroke where your hair never gets wet, but that's about it. There was a swimming certificate on the wall in the Kaufmann's flat which Ilona had been awarded many years previously in Poland. The Polish word for swimming is *plywanie* which is pronounced the same way as the Slovak word *plivanie*. Unfortunately the Slovak word means 'spitting', so the Kaufmann girls could claim to have a mother who was a champion spitter, causing much amusement all round.

There could be laughter and fun, certainly, but Gerda was not the only one with problems. She was simply the one who showed them the most obviously. Jana was also in a highly traumatised state due to everything that had happened over the last few years, and finds it impossible now to tell me the precise order of the events that followed. Confused or not, she was about to discover, one way or another, that she was not entirely alone.

Maňá had been unable to receive any news since the fall of France when all communications had ceased. Otto, meanwhile, had become well established as an opera singer with a very recognisable voice. This was to prove a key factor in re-establishing communication. One day a friend of Jana's came round to see her and announced excitedly, 'They are in England!' The friend explained that he'd been listening to a *BBC Overseas Service* concert and had

163

recognised Otto's distinctive voice. Otto hadn't been singing under his own name at the time, presumably in order to protect any relations back in Czechoslovakia, but there was no doubting that it was him.

Jana was in the garden with Gerda and Vera one day when Ilona came out. She told the twins to go back indoors. When they'd gone, she sat Jana down on a bench and told her she'd had a letter from Máňa which confirmed that Kamila and Gustav were not on any of the lists of camp survivors. Jana's worst fears were realised. Ilona gave her a hug and left her alone sitting in the garden. She told her daughters to let her be alone for a while. Jana is not sure in retrospect if this was the best thing to do or not. Should she have been left alone to deal with this by herself? My personal view is that Ilona did the right thing. Jana needed some time to absorb this terrible news without having an intermediary telling her what to think or do. That could all come later. The privacy was a kindness – but perhaps for the more gregarious Jana, it would have been better to have someone sitting quietly with her while she tried to take it all in. I don't know.

Not everyone had died. Jana now knew that her brother Pavel was safe. After he'd been liberated from Buchenwald he'd gone to live with one of the few sets of surviving relations – Uncle Viktor, Aunt Miluška and their son Miloš, who had managed to weather the war in Prague. Pavel was now the only person in the family who knew that Jana had been hidden, and in which orphanage. He didn't know at first that the orphanage had moved or that she had left to live with the Kaufmanns, so the process took longer than it might have done otherwise to find her, but he managed it eventually. Having found out Jana was okay, he had set out to see if he could rediscover Maňá. He decided to write to Otto c/o the Czechoslovak embassy in London, hoping that because of Otto's status as a professional opera singer, somebody there might be able to give him some information. He wasn't to know this, but Máňa was working at the embassy at this time, so she saw the letter as soon as it arrived and got in touch immediately. She'd known Pavel had survived because he was on the Buchenwald list, but hadn't had any idea of where he was until she came upon his letter. At this point, she'd assumed Jana must be dead as she hadn't been on any of the lists of survivors. It wasn't until the letter from Pavel arrived that she discovered her little sister, now a teenager, whom she hadn't seen since she was nine years old, had been a hidden child and had been saved that way.

Of their friends from the early days, they managed to find out that the Čermaks and Vlaďá Rybák had survived, but Ivan Čermak later told Jana that Mr Rybák, Vláďa's father and a colleague of Gustav's at ČKD had committed suicide after the war. It's not known why. Jana thinks it highly unlikely that he was a collaborator, though that was a common cause of suicide at the time. Vláďa himself left for Prague soon after the war and Jana didn't hear from him again. Her parents, her oldest brother, and virtually all her uncles and aunts had been deported and were now dead. The only relations who had managed to survive in Prague itself were Uncle Viktor and his family. Out of what had originally been a huge family, Uncle Karel had managed to get to the States, and Aunt Herma from Vienna had managed to get to Israel with her sons, but nobody else of the extended family was left.

School had broken up for the summer and Ilona had suggested the girls might all like to go off to a summer camp in the mountains, at a town called Brezová Pod Bradlem. The family had found a larger apartment and were getting ready to move into it, so it the holiday camp was suggested as a perfect way to move without the girls getting under everyone's feet, quite apart from any other reasons. They also thought it would be a good idea for the girls to start mixing with other children who had not had such a traumatic time during the war. Gerda hated to hear the word 'camp'. It made her think work camp, concentration camp, extermination camp. It terrified her. It took a very patient

Hugo to explain that this was a play camp, whether they would hike in the woods, swim in the lakes and get good food. Gerda was also suffering separation anxiety again, but Vera was keen to go. She told the others it would be great – all that freedom!

They were driven to the camp in a special bus and even Gerda had to admit it was a jolly trip. Their accommodation was in rows of attractive chalet style huts. The days were full of organised activities, and they soon all cheered up. After a fortnight of swimming, camping, orientation by starlight, and various games, there were two unexpected visitors – Maňá and Ilona. It seemed Maňá had sprung into action once she knew where both Pavel and Jana were living. She had travelled directly to Bratislava that summer to organise everything, staying with the Nováks, the friends of her youth, who still lived in the very apartment block over the showroom where Jana had been born. Maňá had arranged to crate up and transport those goods from their parents' old home that had been hidden in the cellar. This consisted mostly of a good china dinner service, a number of books, and some rugs. I know this china dinner service well – it always used to come out when we had guests at home. As I only have to pick up a piece of posh crockery and it cracks, I'm always amazed that this beautiful fine china managed to survive the war without a single breakage.

Jana doesn't know where Gustav's stamp collection was hidden, but Maňá managed to ship everything else she could find back to London. This done, she and Jana now left for Prague where they joined Pavel with Uncle Viktor's family. They had to sleep on the floor because of the lack of space, but they'd soon be on the move again so this didn't matter. Having sorted out the transportation of various goods, Máňa now needed to turn her attention to sorting out her brother and sister and finding them somewhere permanent to live. She left Jana and Pavel in Prague, and returned to London to organise the transport. They were to be two of 'the boys'; a transport initiative that is described in great detail in *The Boys* by Sir Martin Gilbert. This was the organised movement of concentration camp survivors and orphans. The British government had said they would take up to a thousand of the youngsters – not permanently, but to gather them together in one place in order to send them out to any surviving relations who could care for them, whether in Israel, the States, or anywhere else. They couldn't find one thousand orphans as so few had survived, so the total number was around three hundred. There were many more boys than girls; hence the title of the book.

The arrangements were completed, and Jana and Pavel set off. This was not to be the easiest of journeys. On 13th August 1945, ten Stirling bombers of 196 Squadron set off for Prague to collect the children. They returned the following evening. Originally, twenty-two planes were going to be used, with sixteen children per aircraft, but in the event only half that number flew as bad weather was closing in at Prague and it was becoming unsafe to fly. The planes had not been adapted for passengers, so there was no seating for the children and they had to huddle together on sacks on the floor, crammed in tightly as there were so few planes. The turbulence was bad. One of the airmen tried to explain what the paper bags were for. He could only speak English, which wasn't very useful, but luckily one boy – a young lad from Yugoslavia – had a basic knowledge of the language. This boy couldn't speak Czech or Polish, however, so that didn't get them much further. Most of the children on the transport were Polish, with only a few Czechs. The Yugoslav boy translated from English into Serbo-Croat, which helped a bit, but in the end everyone understood from the airman's miming what the paper bags were for. They no doubt hoped they wouldn't be necessary.

No such luck – it really was stormy, and they were packed into the bomber like sardines, sitting on the floor with their paper bags and throwing up most of the way. Jana managed by sheer willpower not to be sick. I couldn't have managed it, not with kids vomiting all around me and the plane battling the turbulence. I don't know how long it took them to get from Prague to Holland, their first stopping off point, but I'm sure it felt too long. The stop for re-fuelling at least gave the children a much needed short break for some fresh air, but all too soon it was back on the plane for the final stretch to the Lake District.

Once they'd landed at RAF Crosby-on-Eden (now Carlisle Lake District Airport) they were transferred to a series of buses and army trucks that had been co-opted to take them to their accommodation. The last transport left the airfield at 10.30pm. The truck Jana and Pavel were travelling in broke down, so they didn't arrive at the hostel until the early hours of the following morning. On arrival, they were immediately inspected to see if they needed de-lousing or worse. Finally they were allowed a shower and could retire to bed. This was absolute bliss for the children; a clean bed in a single room. So many of them had been living in dormitories or huge barracks in concentration camps, or on sacks of potatoes in cellars that to suddenly be given white sheets in a room of their own was wonderful. The immigration officer commented on the exceptionally good behaviour of the children and the fact that all instructions were immediately obeyed. I suspect they were all too exhausted and bewildered to even think of doing anything else.

This hostel accommodation they were using was in the wartime village of Calgarth Estate, near Troutbeck, Windermere. This housing scheme had been built to accommodate workers at the Short Sunderland 'Flying Boat' factory that had been relocated to White Cross Bay, the original factory in Rochester having been seriously damaged in a German bombing raid in 1940. At the end of the war, many of the workers had returned to their homes, which is why the estate was available for the children who were housed in the vacated single workers' hostels. The estate was later demolished, bit by bit, from 1954 onwards. The last buildings were used until 1973.

Jana doesn't think the children were frightened, but many of them had not the slightest idea of what was going on or what was going to happen. Here they were, surrounded by English adults who were clearly well-intentioned but who didn't know how to begin to communicate with the children. In the end the adults decided Yiddish would be the most useful common language. This was fine for most of the Polish children, but no good for Jana and Pavel as they couldn't speak a word of it. German would have been easier, but although there were German speaking adults there, it was probably deemed inappropriate. They all managed somehow.

This was a beautiful place. For children who had spent the last few years in the camps, it must have looked like paradise on earth. They could go for walks, take boats out on the lake. Many couldn't believe that such a place could exist, not after all the horrors they had seen. Food was plentiful, and everyone was nice to them. Some of the local people were particularly kind and invited small groups of the children into their homes, but again, the language barrier stopped any true communication. The chances of finding anyone in Troutbeck or Windermere who spoke Czech or Slovak would be slim even today, but back then it was impossible. Jana felt particularly sorry for some of the younger children – ten year olds who had never even learnt to read because they had spent so much of their lives in concentration camps. The local residents arranged classes to teach a bit of basic English and also do some drawing and painting, as a stress-reliever more than anything else. I suppose we'd call it 'art therapy' today. It can't have done any harm, but at the same time, it was impossible for these people, however good their intentions, to understand the experiences of these children, many of whom were old beyond their years, and all of whom were heavily traumatised. Jana was aware she was one of the lucky ones. Despite the harshness of the regime at the orphanage, at least she didn't have the hideous nightmare memories of the camp survivors.

There were a few other Czechs amongst the youngsters at Troutbeck, so Jana and Pavel mostly socialised with them. It saved trying to work through the communication problems with the others. Amongst this

169

small group was a girl called Kitty Rosen who left for Manchester en route to the States, and a boy called Misha Honigwachs, who came to London and eventually changed his name to Michael Honey. Many names were changed and anglicised, though Jana kept her own, putting up ever since with people calling her 'Yarna' instead of the Czech pronunciation which is more like 'Yanna'.

Their arrival was naturally newsworthy, and at one point a photographer arrived to take pictures, many of which were published in the Picture Post and local newspapers. Pavel is pictured in one of them, sitting on a step with a girl who he thinks was one of the local ones, not one of the transport children. She's tall and healthy looking, so I'm sure he's right. The pictures were a little bit posed, but still a remarkable record. The local girls were a revelation for Pavel – they ran around with the boys, grabbing waists and anything else. He was emphatically not used to this sort of thing.

Jana and Pavel stayed in the Lake District for a further two weeks until it was time to make the last leg of the journey to London, by train. When they arrived, Maňá met them at the station. Jana must have hoped this was the last move. She was beginning to feel like felt like a parcel being pushed from here to there, so much had been happening. Things were not going to be easy – she was in a new country that was completely foreign to her, and all she knew of the language was the scant amount she may have picked up since her arrival a fortnight earlier – but she had a family again. She wasn't alone.

PART THREE

22

ENGLISH AS A FOREIGN LANGUAGE

In London at last, Jana and Pavel joined Maňá and Otto in their small but comfortable two bedroom flat in Chepstow Court, Notting Hill. The flat was opposite a bombsite which the local residents used for a bonfire on 5th November. I've taken a look at the area on Google Streetview – Chepstow Court is still there, a good, solid block of flats, but any bombsites in the area have been long since built over with low rise flats and small terraced houses. I suspect it is now a far more expensive place to live in than it was in the forties.

The first priority for Jana and Pavel was to learn English, so they enrolled at the Regent Street Polytechnic, now the University of Westminster, for a full-time course in *English as a Foreign Language*. They were joined by one of the boys they'd become friendly with at Troutbeck – Misha Honigwachs. Jana was sure he fancied her, judging by his very friendly behaviour when they went to the cinema together. Misha was also living with relations in London, along with another boy from the transport.

The polytechnic was located in Upper Regent Street, with an annexe nearby where the EFL classes were held. Jana, Paul and Misha were the youngest there, as most of the others students on the course were ex-members of the Polish Army in Exile and RAF personnel. These men referred to Jana and the other youngsters as 'the children', but Jana didn't let their patronising attitude get to her. As always, she studied hard and impressed her teachers. After learning enough English to continue her education in her new language, she embarked upon a two year Matriculation course, also at the Regent Street Polytechnic, but this time in the main part of the college. Many of the students were ex-army again, but there were also a number of young people who had been evacuated during the war and were returning to their education after the long interruption.

Pavel didn't join Jana on this course as he was waiting for a visa to go to the States, but Misha and another boy from the transport had no immediate plans to leave so were still studying. The food in the polytechnic's canteen impressed Jana as being remarkably cheap. A main course cost as little as a shilling, and dessert was only sixpence. After a period of intensive study, she matriculated in 1948/9 in English, Maths, Russian, Geography and Czech, which was an incredible achievement for someone who had arrived in England just a few years earlier speaking no English. I doubt if she even spoke it at home with Maňá and Otto. Certainly when I was a child and used to visit Auntie Maňá and Uncle Otto, my mother would immediately launch into Czech conversation with them – most annoying, when I'd hear my name mentioned and not know what they were saying.

As soon as she had a reasonable amount of English fluency, Jana started writing to her Uncle Karel and his wife Elizabeth about her experiences at the polytechnic.

... As you perhaps know, I am now studying for the London University Matriculation. I have quite a lot to do, I am busy the whole day. At school I am three hours in the morning and three in the afternoon, besides we get plenty of homeworks and so I have little time for something else. The most difficult subject for me is English. Sometimes we have to rewrite a paragraph which is in Shakespearean English, in modern idiomatic English. It happens that some words are not to be found even in a dictionary, so how can I know them! Well, as every book has its last page, I hope I shall get through to the end of our next book too. Geography is not easy either, we take everything in detail, but it is nothing in

174

comparison with English. Mathematics, however, I find quit easy, for I have learnt once almost everything we take now.

Some of my time is also spent with my little nephew, although I do nothing with him. I sometimes just look at him. Few people would believe that so small a baby can be amusing but he really is, and I simply love him.

The principal of the matric course at the Polytechnic, Mr Moon, occasionally asked for Jana's help in sorting books in his office during the lunch break. He couldn't giver her money for this, so she was rewarded with books, such as John Buchan's *The Thirty-nine Steps*.

She kept busy, and kept writing to Karel and Elizabeth. Their daughter Marian preserved these letters, and they give a real taste of what life was like at the time for Jana:

... I am now rather busy with my school work. I don't remember if I wrote to you about my first examination in an ordinary English school. The report was surprisingly good. Just imagine that in an almost all-English class I, a foreigner, was the second best in English! I could not believe my eyes. I am sure they had someone else in their mind when they wrote my report; it must have been a case of mistaken identity.

As I said before, I am quite busy. I come home from school at about five o'clock except on Tuesday when I have evening classes and on Wednesday when I go in the evening to the "Sokol". We get always plenty of homeworks and although I do some of them in school, (which is, of course, against the rules,) there always remains something to be done at home. This, naturally, leaves me little time to play with little Charles, though I like playing with him very much for he is a very sweet baby. He is also very pretty, he has lovely big blue eyes, red cheeks, and when he is not sleeping or eating he is usually smiling, sometimes even laughing.

On the day after tomorrow I am going to a hospital to have my tonsils taken out at last. You can't imagine how I am looking forward to it. (I don't mean the operation but the time when I have no more troubles with my throat.) Thank God that in England even as slight an operation as this is done under anaesthetic. I have already prepared several books to take with me to the hospital for I am a great reader; I read normally ten books a week (that's a slight exaggeration) so I think that in the hospital, where I shall be able to read the whole day, the number of books needed will be at least doubled.

I've seen some of Jana's certificates and reports from this period and just like her earlier school reports, they make for impressive reading. In June 1946 she took the University of Cambridge Local Examinations Syndicate Lower Certificate in English and gained a B in Dictation, Reading and Conversation, an A in Translation from and into English, and an A in English Composition and Language. In July and August that same year, she took the Polytechnic School of Modern Language's Advanced Stage of English, Written & Oral, and was awarded a first class certificate.

Her reports for that year confirm how well she was working. The comments for English read – *Work of high standard. Should do very well*; Geography – *Excellent work*; Mathematics – *A capable student*; and in General Remarks – *She is an exceptionally good student in all her work. She promises to do very well indeed.*

The trend continued in the reports that followed. In July 1947, comments include: English – *An exemplary student*; Geography – *Excellent work*; Mathematics – *A keen worker*; General Remarks – *She is an outstanding student. Her power of concentration is remarkable and her work always of the highest quality.* December 1947: English – *Has an excellent command of this subject*; Geography – *an exemplary student*; Mathematics – *An excellent term's work*; General Remarks: *Her work always teaches a high standard. She is one of the best students the Department has ever had.*

And finally in July 1948: English – *An intelligent student. Should do well*; Geography – *Should be very successful*; Mathematics – *Excellent work throughout the year*; General Remarks – *She is an excellent student and makes meritorious progress. Her other two subjects are outside our curriculum, but she works very hard at these also. She is one of our best students and never varies from a very high standard of achievement.*

Her University of London certificate states that she matriculated at the June Examination in the year 1948, and was placed in the First Division, having satisfied the Examiners in English, Elementary Mathematics, Russian, Czechoslovak, Geography. The following year she took the mathematics further and gained a First Class Certificate in Arithmetic, Advanced Stage, from the Royal Society for the Encouragement of Arts Manufactures and Commerce, London, studying for this at the North-Western Polytechnic, London.

Pavel, in the meantime, was working at first in a radio shop and later on at a farm in Essex, spending his free time at the cinema while he waited for his visa to come through. He had been invited by his mother's brother, Karel Löwner, to live with him and his wife Elisabeth in the United States.

On 9th October 1946, Pavel wrote this letter to Karel.

When I was 17th September at the American consulate, they told me that all documents are in order but that it can take also six months, before I get the visa. I thought I would be able to get the visa soon after visiting the consulate. But I am sorry that it did not materialise. So perhaps I will not be able to visit the second course, which you suggested in your last letter. Perhaps I could get visa as a student. I will try it that way.

To-morrow I am going for some time to a farm. It will do me good to get some fresh air and do some physical work

Now I cannot go to any school because they are full and also they take students only for longer time than I could afford.

177

For the first time I write an English letter to you. I think that there are many mistakes in it but I hope that you will understand it.

Karel was a professor at Syracuse University by this time. The little boy who had lain on the floor imagining chess games had come a long way. At age ten, he had joined his older siblings in Prague to attend the Gymnasium as education beyond 5th grade was not available in Lány. This of course had set the precedent for Jirka to do the same thing with tragic results later on. Karel went on to obtain a multitude of qualifications and posts: PhD Prague, 1917; Asst. maths. German Engineering School, Prague 1917-22; Privatdozent, Berlin. 1922-28; Asst. Prof. Cologne 1928-30; Prague 1930-33; Ordentlicher Professor 1933-39; Lecturer Louisville Univ. 1939-42; Asst. Prof. 1942-44; Research Assoc. Brown Univ 1944-45; Assoc. Prof. Syracuse Univ; Prof. Syracuse Univ 1946-51; eventually ending up at Stanford University. 1951-68.

Apparently he had originally considered medicine as a career, but changed his mind after a visit to a mortuary. He married Elisabeth Alexander in March 1934. When the couple emigrated to the US in 1939, Karel had to take a lowly job as an elementary school teacher, though he also gave free advanced maths lessons in a brewery of all the unlikely places. Once his skills and reputation were recognised, he managed to obtain the professorship at Brown University. In 1946, he moved to Syracuse. Later, in 1950, he would move to Stanford, which was then the centre of the world for mathematical analysis. I have some lecture notes from Pavel that describe exactly what he was doing there mathematically, but as a non-mathematician I don't understand a word of it, so all I can say is he became prolific in research into monotonic matrix functions and applications to fluid dynamics, invariant measures of Hilbert spaces, operators in quantum mechanics, partial differential equations, geometric function theory of complex variables, differential geometry, continuous groups and Lie

178

semigroups, etc. I have no idea what any of that means, but if you're a mathematician and are reading this I hope you're nodding wisely in recognition.

He worked at Stanford until his death in 1968. Maňá wrote this letter to her cousin Marian, on 21st Jan 1968.

I can hardly tell you what this loss means to me. Your father was my favourite uncle and I have many memories of him since my early childhood. I remember how patiently he stood up to my pestering him when I played at mother and child with him; needless to say that I was the mother and he my little boy. I combed his hair endlessly and commanded him, until grandmother had to beg me to leave him in peace. But he was always game to my imagination, and now I feel I lost with him part of my life.

I have put a more detailed account of Karel and Elisabeth's life in America in the appendix.

Pavel eventually managed to obtain his visa and made the journey to the States where, like so many other émigrés, he Anglicised his name, changing it from Pavel Graf to Paul Graf Loewner (the Anglicised spelling of Löwner). Karel had also Anglicised his name and was now known as Charles Loewner, but I'll still refer to him as 'Karel' as to me he'll always be 'Uncle Karel'. Pavel, however, has always been 'Uncle Paul' as far as I'm concerned, so I'll use 'Paul' from now on. He took to the high level of education now available with relish. After graduating from Syracuse, he also taught at Stanford before pursuing a successful career at IBM in New York. Karel had been friendly many years earlier with Albert Einstein, and now Paul followed the family tradition of hobnobbing with exceptional mathematicians by sharing a taxi to work with the eminent mathematician Benoit Mandelbrot – he who coined the word 'fractal'. It was while he was working at IBM in 1979 that Mandelbrot was to discover the Mandelbrot Set, *one of the*

179

most astonishing discoveries in the entire history of mathematics according to Arthur C Clarke.

Gustav and Kamila would have been delighted with their children's academic achievements. I'm amazed particularly at how quickly my mother was able to learn English. I know immersion in the language is the best way to learn it, but even so, I'm not sure I would have felt able to take exams in so many subjects so soon in a language I had only been speaking for a couple of years. I can't help thinking my natural laziness would have kicked in and I'd have gone and done something that didn't require such sheer hard work. My mother was not, however, destined to have an academic career. Such things would have been unusual for a woman at that time. She had some thoughts of what she could do career-wise – teaching perhaps – but first of all she had to have some basic training in something practical that could get her a job.

23

THE LONDON PALLADIUM

Shortly after coming to London, Maňá had suggested Jana join the Czech gymnastic association, Sokol. Jana already had a friend who was a member – Irena Šnajdrová, who Jana knew from the Regent Street Polytechnic. I'd never heard of Sokol before Mother mentioned it in her notes to me, but the name kept popping up so I did some research. They were an interesting organisation: founded in Prague back in 1862, they quickly spread through the Austro-Hungarian Empire and beyond. Many people saw them as an early precursor to the scouting movement, though they were in essence very different. Sokol's ideological roots lay in the physical training of athletes and warriors established in Ancient Greece. The organisation was officially disbanded in 1915, but this didn't stop them later flourishing in the period between the wars. That revival came to an abrupt halt when they were brutally suppressed by the Nazis in Bohemia and Moravia. They re-emerged after the war only to be banned by yet again by the Communists, but they had better luck abroad. The emigration of Sokol members and the setting up of groups overseas had been going on since 1918, which is why it was easy for Jana to find a group in London although it would have been impossible back in Prague or Bratislava. The group she joined met once a week in a school in Notting Hill Gate for a mixture of music and movement, simple apparatus work and folk dancing. They weren't just a once a week 'keep fit' club, as they also put on displays of exercises and folk dances, usually at the Czech club in West

Hampstead or other nearby social clubs. Other venues were more prestigious – Jana took part in larger scale international displays including choreographed exercises to music at the Albert Hall, and dancing in national costume at the London Palladium.

I couldn't believe what I was hearing. My mother had danced at the London Palladium? How had I not known this? It sounded so unlikely. More research was needed. I checked the history. At around the time my Mother danced there, Val Parnell had taken over the running of the London Palladium and was busy booking top American acts like Danny Kaye and Mickey Rooney. Mother is not now, and never has been a top American act, so I didn't understand how she could have appeared on that particular stage. I rang her up to ask about this. The answer was simple: from Monday to Saturday, the London Palladium was a glittering showcase of international stars, but on a Sunday it could be taken over by anyone with the wherewithal to book such a huge theatre – hence the folk dancing. This was part of a much larger entertainment with many different groups taking part: a one day showcase for various gymnastic groups under the *Health and Strength* banner. The Sokol members performed some exercises to music as well as folk dances in national costumes. This would have been in 1947 or thereabouts. There was a similar show in the Albert Hall a year later, and as I've now seen a photo of the Palladium performance, I'm in no doubt that it all happened exactly as I've been told.

Sokol wasn't just about physical education, it was also about meeting like-minded people and socialising generally. Maruška, one of Jana's new friends from Sokol, introduced her to a family who needed a baby-sitter, which was a handy way for her to earn some extra pocket money. Maruška was also instrumental in arranging for Jana to appear in other stage performances. Her husband fancied himself as a theatrical producer and put on a Czech folk play, *Švanda the Bagpiper* at the Czech Club. Jana played a wood nymph in this production. I'm trying to imagine my

182

mother as a wood nymph. It's almost as hard as imagining her dancing at the Palladium, but Mother is full of surprises. She also played the angel who accompanies St Nicholas during the St Nicholas festivities on 6th December. I had no idea about any of this until she sent me the notes about this part of her life. In more recent times, I was aware that she had joined the local amateur dramatic club, the Wickham Court Players, but this was as wardrobe mistress, not actor, so I've never seen her on stage as such. The closest thing to my mother performing that I've witnessed has been the 'keep fit' displays that she occasionally took part in during the sixties. At least all that Sokol training was put to good use. For a while, she even ran her own 'keep fit' evening classes, based on similar techniques of doing exercises to music. I occasionally accompanied her to these classes, probably during school half term holidays. She took a portable gramophone and a handful of records down to the local Assembly Rooms where she taught exercises to music to a class of interested ladies. The exercises in question were about stretching more than aerobics, and many were similar to the sort of thing shown on fitness TV programmes of the time. One in particular I recall, as Mother had bought the book of the show, was *Boomph With Becker*. Many of these exercises were the sort that you're given dire warnings about nowadays as they're supposed to cripple you for life, but I don't recall anyone ever injuring themselves in my mother's classes. Needless to say, the supposedly back-breaking physical jerks were done to mostly classical music, such as excerpts from Holst's *The Planets*. Whenever I hear *Jupiter* nowadays I can't help but see a group of ladies swinging their arms and touching their toes.

Irena Šnajdrová, who had introduced Jana to Sokol, was shortly to be married and asked Jana to be her bridesmaid. She was arranging the wedding on a shoestring so couldn't afford to provide a bridesmaid's dress. Jana didn't want to spend a lot of money on something she would wear only once, but managed to find a way round this. She had a work colleague called Gladys Gardner, known as

'Gee-Gee' behind her back, who was only slightly taller but of similar build, and needed a dress for a ball. The obvious solution was to buy one between them, so a full length pale blue dress was duly purchased. Jana wore it to the wedding in a Roman Catholic Church and then passed the dress on to her work colleague. Irena's wedding took place on a freezing day, so Jana wore a woolly vest under the flimsy dress. When I first read that in Mother's notes, my first thought was, 'I hope it didn't show', but I needn't have worried. I've now seen a photo of the occasion, and the dress looks lovely. No thermals on view at all.

Prancing about on famous stages and gaining qualifications wouldn't have been possible without the security of knowing she had her own room to return to in the flat at Chepstow Court. This couldn't be a permanent arrangement, however. In 1946 Máňa had given birth to a baby boy, Charles George, named after his two late uncles, Otto's brother Karel (no relation to the other Uncle Karel), and Maňá's brother Jirka.

Máňa wrote to Elisabeth, the other Uncle Karel's wife, on Oct 6th 1946.

Thank you also for the precious parcel of baby things. Believe me, it was really most welcome, as all the baby clothes are on coupons, the amount of which is not very great. I am sure you will understand how busy I was in the last few weeks; first I was looking desperately for a bigger flat – unfortunately in rain – and it was a full time job indeed; then all the preparations for the "event", and if you add all the work in the household, you surely will see that I got sometimes so tired that I was just unable to do some more work, if it was "only" writing a letter. And now the baby arrived, fortunately without any difficulties and quickly, and I am now naturally even more busy than ever before. (On top of everything I am left just now without a help, as my charwoman got ill and is in hospital.) Well, anyhow, my son – Charles George – is, "of course", quite a miracle as every baby. He was actually very tiny, but now he

184

is gaining according to plan. I think he is very much like Otto. To watch him is really a terrific thrill....! I arrived from the hospital after ten days and the troubles with the space started, but with some patience we manage somehow.

Jana had to share a room with the infant Charles at first, but at least she could make herself useful as a live-in babysitter. Sharing with a young baby was all very well, but once she was feeling more confident and independent, and had a job enabling her to support herself, she moved into her own flat – a tiny bedsit just a few doors down in a Victorian terrace.

Meanwhile, back in Chepstow Court, the layout of the flat meant the inevitable had happened and they had been burgled. The kitchen window had a flimsy catch and a fire escape immediately beneath it, which would have been useful in the event of fire, but was also an obvious security risk. Realising the dangers, Maňá and Otto had taken to locking the kitchen door whenever they went out. This proved to be a sensible precaution as they were burgled one day shortly before Christmas when they'd gone to the cinema to see Powell and Pressburger's latest film, *I Know Where I'm Going!* Foodstuffs were still being rationed at that time so Maňá had been meticulously saving any spare butter, sugar, and dried fruit for her Christmas baking. All of this was stolen, along with a pair of shoes that had been left in the kitchen to be cleaned. Fortunately the burglar couldn't get beyond the kitchen, so nothing too precious was lost.

24

OPERA

Living with Otto and Maňá meant Jana was bound to come into contact with the cultural elite; the writers, artists and musicians who moved in their set in London. Among the writers was Jiři Mucha, son of the Art Nouveau artist Alphonse. Otto and Maňá had known Mucha well in Paris, of course, but much had changed since then. He had joined the newly formed Czech army in Agde, but after the fall of France had come to England and joined the Czech section of the RAF, later becoming a BBC war correspondent. His first wife, Vitezslava had died in 1940, and he had recently married the Scottish musician Geraldine Thomsen. Geraldine's father was a professor at the Royal Academy of Music, and through him Geraldine had met the composers Rachmaninov, Elgar and Strauss. I'm permitting myself a few moments of composer-envy here. I studied composition at music college myself, but never met anyone in that sort of league. Geraldine was busy with musical arrangements rather than writing original material when Jana knew her, but later she became a respected composer in her own right. I've read that in her old age she explained she had become a composer to take her mind off things when her husband was arrested by the Communists. Geraldine's mother was also part of the arty set in London and took Jana under her wing, escorting her to a multitude of art galleries. This lady spoke with a strong Scottish accent which was barely comprehensible to Jana at the time, as she'd only just learnt English, but she appreciated the attention and the art.

With Otto being a leading opera singer, most of the 'arty' people Jana met were the eminent musicians of the day, so it's impossible for me to avoid a certain amount of name-dropping. Among others, she met the opera singers Joan Cross, Edgar Evans and Peter Pears – and the composer Benjamin Britten. She met Britten in Aldeburgh, where Otto and Maňá were on holiday. Jana had come down for the weekend, having been at a concert the night before in the Albert Hall in which she had heard Britten's *Serenade for Tenor, Horn and Strings*. When Jana told Britten how much she had liked the piece, he said he was surprised that a teenage girl who wasn't even a musician had enjoyed it. I'm sure her love for the music was genuine, however, as it's a piece she's often mentioned to me as being a favourite, quite outside the context of the first hearing.

Through Otto and Maňá she also met the ballet dancer Leo Kersley and his wife, the writer Janet Sinclair. They took Jana to see ballet performances where she could relax and enjoy the music and the drama without needing any knowledge of English. I met Leo Kersley once. He must be the only one of these famous people I've actually spoken to. I've seen Peter Pears in concert, but that doesn't count as we didn't even say hello, but Mother and I were at a WEA weekend course on ballet in the De La Warr Pavilion at Bexhill on Sea many years ago, and we bumped into Leo halfway down a staircase. Mother had a quick chat with him and introduced me. I knew he was one of the lecturers on the course, but had no idea at the time of how my mother knew him.

For her twenty-first birthday, the Kersleys gave Jana a book of opera stories, hoping she'd manage to see them all by the time she was forty-two. She nearly managed it.

Now that she was twenty-one, Jana was eligible to apply for naturalisation. She needed two sponsors so asked Leo Kersley to be one. He would have been happy to oblige except that he didn't think this would be a good idea as he was a member of the Communist Party and had been a conscientious objector during the war. He had a point, so

187

Jana turned instead to her director at work, Walter Hindes Godfrey CBE, FSA, FRIBA. Never mind the other qualifications: a Commander of the British Empire certainly sounds more suitable for the purpose than someone with Communist Party membership papers. She duly achieved naturalisation.

As a child, Jana had read stories by the Dutch author Johan Fabricius, and now she was lucky enough to meet him, as he was yet another of Otto and Maňá's friends. Indonesian born Fabricius was also an artist, having trained as a realist figurative painter at the Academy of Art in The Hague. This may have accounted for his powers of observation and description which made his children's books so popular with youngsters like my mother. He had three children of his own, and Jana admits to having been quite keen on his eldest for a while; a music student called Janeiko.

On 12th July, 1946, Glyndebourne re-opened with the world première of Benjamin Britten's opera *The Rape of Lucretia.* Otto was singing the role of Tarquinius, and Maňá and Jana were both present at the dress rehearsal. This opera was not initially the success that might have been expected, given that Britten had enjoyed international plaudits with *Peter Grimes* just one year earlier. *Lucretia* was a very different work. Britten had deliberately written it as a chamber opera as the forces required to stage *Grimes* made it prohibitively expensive to mount in a time of austerity. *Lucretia,* being on a smaller scale, was designed to be more attractive to opera companies. It had a stellar cast on its opening night, including Kathleen Ferrier and Peter Pears, and many people loved it – but others were more critical. One of its supporters was the musicologist and critic John W Klein, who would describe it in an article in *Musical Opinion* magazine three years later as containing unforgettable moments and flashes of genius which made it comparable to the best of Verdi. Sounds good to me, but while in Klein's view it had more real drama than many English operas of the time, which should have helped it to succeed, it would be many years until it finally gained the reputation it deserved.

The original production went on a lengthy and not entirely successful tour, which produced real financial problems for the company, but at least one of the performances was recorded. The performance in question took place in October that year in Amsterdam. I'm listening to the performance, re-issued on CD, as I write this. The actual quality of the recording is a bit rough but it's still giving me plenty of shiver-down-the-spine moments when I realise I'm writing about something I can still hear, exactly as it happened. Otto was never keen on studio recordings and made very few, so this one's a real bonus as far as I'm concerned. More and more pirated copies of his performances are turning up these days, presumably recorded by amateurs from live radio broadcasts, and now available commercially.

Whatever the critics and general public may have felt about *Lucretia*, for Jana, after the years of no music or culture, this must have been nothing short of a miracle – being present at a performance of cutting edge contemporary music of the highest quality with her brother-in-law singing the lead baritone part, and her sister at her side. It was also a reminder of her love for opera which had been nurtured during those childhood visits to the National Theatre to watch the Sunday matinées in what must have felt like a lifetime ago. To make up for lost time, she now went to opera after opera; she couldn't get enough of them. A highlight came two years later, when Jana accompanied Máňa and the infant Charles to Amsterdam to see Otto in a performance of *The Flying Dutchman* with the Amsterdam Opera. This was her first experience of Wagner, but unlike Gustav, who'd snoozed all the way through *Parsifal*, she was not going to sleep through a minute. My infant cousin Charles probably wouldn't have slept through it either, but he might have been noisier than was appropriate. Luckily a friend in the opera company, Rientje Cohen, was on hand to organise the babysitting. Rientje was the opera company's secretary at the time. Her husband Eddie taught at the university and arranged for one of his students, a young man called Wim Wimmers to take Jana around Amsterdam during her stay. As well as the museums and art galleries, Jana recalls Wim showing her his room in a dilapidated house where his bed was stood on bricks to keep it level, and a bucket collected rainwater in one corner. Sounds like typical student digs. Eddie and Rientje would later move to the US, where Eddie became professor of theoretical physics at the Rockefeller institute.

In 1948, the eminent Czech conductor Rafael Kubelik was invited to Britain by the Glyndebourne Opera Company on the recommendation of Bruno Walther. He was booked to take *Don Giovanni* on tour to Scotland for the fledgling Edinburgh Festival. Kubelik duly arrived, together with his wife and small son. He had made arrangements for an English girl to look after the little boy while he was in Britain but the girl had fallen ill. Otto recommended Jana as a substitute and the recommendation was accepted. This gave Jana a memorable summer. She looked after two year old Martin Kubelik both at Glyndebourne during rehearsals, and later in Edinburgh, where the toddler was dragged all around the city so that Jana could go sightseeing. I doubt if he has any recollection of this. It's a shame that it's so hard to have a clear impression of anything that happened when you were just two years old. Martin later went on to study architecture, so perhaps something of the city's atmosphere impinged on his infant mind. I was in Edinburgh only last week. I love that place – the way the tall buildings reflect the sudden hills, the castle, Princes Street gardens, Waverley station. It's unforgettable, and quite unlike anywhere else. I wondered if it would be possible to contact Martin after all these years, so went for a search for him on the internet. The great thing about academics is that they always have handy websites with email addresses that work. I wrote to him with some trepidation, not sure if I'd even found the right Professor Martin Kubelik, but luckily I had, and he was

190

delighted to be contacted. The photos of his infant self as a little scrap of a lad are a startling contrast to the photos one can find on the internet of the tall bearded professor of architecture.

Jana was an attractive young woman with a charming foreign accent, so it's no great surprise that one of the singers on the Edinburgh trip tried to lure her into his hotel bedroom. He claimed it was because he had something for little Martin, but Jana, wisely, pretended not to understand enough English to know what he was saying. She has since told me exactly who he was, but I think discretion is in order here, even though nothing untoward happened.

To entertain Martin, Jana got into the habit of taking him to some of the rehearsals. He appeared to enjoy them, but this backfired one time. The Italian bass/baritone, Vito de Taranto, who was there to sing Leporello in Mozart's *Don Giovanni*, liked to make animal noises to amuse the little boy. During the dress rehearsal, which Jana and her young charge attended, little Martin recognised Vito when he appeared on stage and started making loud animal noises at him. The singers all reacted with surprise, and no doubt amusement, but this most important rehearsal had been interrupted. Jana jumped up and took Martin out as quickly as she could. Excessive animal impressions may have taken their toll on Vito – who knows – as later on the tour he lost his voice. He still acted the role, but the singing was done by Erich Kunz from the wings.

25

THE NATIONAL BUILDINGS RECORD

When she returned to London after the Edinburgh trip, Jana embarked upon a secretarial course at the North Western Polytechnic, Prince of Wales Road, NW5, in Camden Town, now part of London Metropolitan University. She worked hard and did well, learning typing, shorthand and associated skills. I have seen some of the certificates for tests she took for the class teacher in shorthand and typing, and they include one hundred words per minute in a four minute shorthand test, and forty-five words per minute in a ten minutes typewriting speed test. The final typing exam, however, was one of the very few exams she ever failed, but this was due to a faulty typewriter rather than any shortcomings in her typing. She complained, but nothing was done, so that was that. In the end, it didn't matter as on completion of the course, the teacher, who knew how good she was really, recommended her to Cecil Farthing FSA (Fellow of the Society of Antiquaries), who was the Deputy Director of the National Buildings Record, later renamed the National Monuments Record, and now part of English Heritage. The Director at this time was Walter Godfrey, CBE, an architect who had been involved in restoration work of City churches after WW2, including Temple Church. Jana's starting salary in 1949 was £4-10s.0d, on which she had to pay a few pence tax. Cecil Farthing was Jana's immediate boss and was also the secretary of the BAA (British Archaeological Association) for whom he organised outings and lectures. Jana's job included helping to organise the itineraries for the outings and photographs for lectures.

The National Buildings Record had been established in 1940 to record buildings of national importance that were thought to be at risk of damage or destruction due to military action, so was essentially a photographic library of buildings of major architectural and historical interest, mainly pre-20th century. It shared buildings with the Royal Commission of the Historical Monuments of England, though initially it was a separate organisation. Rather wonderfully, the two gentlemen who worked in the darkroom on these premises were called Mr Power and Mr Light. Jana's work was varied. When she wasn't doing straightforward secretarial tasks, she helped in the library annotating, indexing and mounting photographs and filing them in boxes arranged by counties. These records were frequently consulted by students of architecture and writers, so once again Jana was coming into contact with famous names. Among the regular visitors were the poet and conservationist John Betjeman, and architectural historian Nikolaus Pevsner. Most of the photographs in Pevsner's *Buildings of England* series came from the NBR archives. Pevsner always announced when he was going to be visiting, so the secretaries had time to get in some good quality biscuits for him, rather than the usual 'dog biscuits' as Cecil Farthing called digestives. The very formal and correct Nikolaus Pevsner was always referred to as 'Herr Professor'.

Occasionally Jana left the premises to accompany the draughtswoman when she was sent to survey a building that was about to be demolished or rebuilt. The two of them would go away for a couple of days and Jana would assist by holding one end of the tape measure or counting brick courses, so nothing very technical, but it must have been nice to get out of the office every now and again.

She had to work alternate Saturdays, so to compensate for this the lunch break was generous at more than an hour. When the NBR was still in South Kensington, this gave her the opportunity to visit the Victoria and Albert

Museum, or pop into Harrods, not to shop so much as to wander around and dream. There were also numerous second-hand bookshops in the vicinity for browsing. South Kensington was very convenient for the Royal Albert Hall, so during the summer Prom season, Jana and a few friends could go directly from work to stand in the queue for promenade tickets. After the concert, she could walk back across the park to the flat at Notting Hill. When the NBR later moved to the edge of Regents Park the workers missed these facilities, but they were replaced by walks in the park.

Jana was keen theatre goer and would happily stand in queues for the cheap tickets for as long as it took. On some of these outings she was accompanied by her then boyfriend, Felix Altschul, which no doubt made the queuing a pleasant experience and helped to pass the time. Felix was a Czech with part Jewish ancestry who had come to England after the war, not as a refugee, but to study. His father was Jewish, but his mother was a Roman Catholic, as was Felix. Jana had met him at the Regent Street Polytechnic when she was doing her matriculation course. They'd soon become good friends, going to the cinema and concerts, but sticking to light classical music as Felix wasn't keen on anything too heavy. Once, for his birthday, Jana treated him to a performance of Mahler's *Das Lied von der Erde* with Kathleen Ferrier singing at the Royal Albert Hall. Lovers of the heavier classics would drool at such an opportunity, but Jana doesn't think Felix was very impressed.

Felix lived with his uncle and aunt in Cobham, Surrey, and Jana would often go down there and borrow his aunt's bicycle so that they could explore the countryside together. The relationship was friendly, but I don't get the impression it went much further than that. Jana doesn't appear to have been heartbroken when Felix eventually emigrated to the US, leaving her his collection of Upton Sinclair novels. He had decided, no doubt sensibly, that entering the States with a collection of extremely left wing books during the Communist witch hunts might not be the cleverest thing to do. I devoured those absorbing novels in

194

my teens, but had no idea until recently that they had once belonged to my mother's boyfriend.

As well as the theatre trips, Jana was still going to the operas as much as she could. As a principal singer, Otto was always given a pair of complimentary tickets for his performances which meant Jana and Maňá attended many first nights. As well as the usual repertoire, they were also at the world première of William Walton's *Troilus and Cressida* at Covent Garden in 1954. This performance apparently suffered from the conductor, the famed Sir Malcom Sargent, not knowing the score as well as he should have done. Another of the premières was Michael Tippett's *The Midsummer Marriage* at Covent Garden in 1955. This one was recorded live, and is available on CD. I know I'm unlikely to hear my mother and aunt coughing or whispering in the audience no such recordings, but it's still nice to know they were there, and I always like to hear my uncle singing. He used to burst into Wagner occasionally in our small living room at home, with my cousin Charles crashing out huge chords on the piano. The sheer volume was terrifying. Wagnerian bass-baritones at close range are far louder than you could possibly imagine.

Just occasionally, Jana actually paid for an opera ticket. When Otto was singing Alberich in *Das Rheingold*, the first part of Wagner's *Ring Cycle*, she was able to see three of the operas on free tickets in the stalls, but Otto didn't appear in *Die Walküre*, the second of the series, so she had to pay for her ticket and see it from high up in the balcony instead. This wasn't the only opera she paid to see. She frequently went to Sadlers Wells where she could sit in what was known as 'the pit' – the back stalls – for about 1/6. She also saw productions by visiting companies from abroad in various London theatres. I know she was also working full time at this point, but it sometimes feels as if her life was one long round of operas and concerts. The contrast with how things had been just a few years earlier in the orphanage is extreme – but the most important difference, far more profound and meaningful than any number of theatre and opera trips, was that she was now living in place where she had a proper family again, and could see them all the time. Years later, after Otto's death in 1980, Jana wrote:

To me he was much more than a brother-in-law and cousin, he was like a combination of second father and elder brother and one of the nicest people I knew.

In later years I witnessed this close relationship, and have to agree – he was one of the nicest people I knew too – funny, kind, generous and very down to earth. Also one of the only people in the family who knew anything about football, a game he loved to watch.

Perhaps the strangest musical 'performance' of any that Jana witnessed was canine rather than human. A cousin of Kamila and Otto's, Hanuš (John) Kraus had left Czechoslovakia before the war, settled in England, married an Englishwoman, and had a daughter a year or so younger than Charles called Audrey – named after the actress Audrey Hepburn. Although it was difficult to acquire anything shortly after the war, he refused Maňá's offers of baby goods that Charles didn't need any more as he felt a new baby had to have everything new. They were not very well off. They later emigrated to the States. Hanuš had a dog, probably a labrador, who apparently played the piano. Jana has a distinct if odd memory of seeing Hanuš at the piano with the dog next to him, hitting the piano keys with his paws. Nowadays he would, of course, be on YouTube for us all to enjoy.

Jana would not be content to remain a shorthand typist all her life however convenient or congenial working at the National Buildings Record might be. The suggestion was made by Karel and Elisabeth over in the States that she might consider furthering her education there by enrolling on a teacher training course. She duly applied to San José College, and asked Professor Moon from Regent Street Polytechnic and her current boss, Cecil Farthing for references, which they were happy to provide.

196

The notes on the reference on the 'Application for Admission to an Educational Institution in the United States' tell the referee that: 'This should be a thoughtful and realistic discrimination between the candidate's strong and weak characteristics, taking into account his character, personality, intellectual ability, emotional stability, adaptability and seriousness of purpose'.

On 5th August, 1954, Professor Moon wrote:

Miss Jana Graf was a full-time day student in the Matriculation (now University Entrance) Department of the Polytechnic, Regent Street, London, W.1., from 17th September, 1946 to 16th July, 1948. She studied English, mathematics, geography, and Russian. Her work was always of the highest quality and it came as no surprise to learn that she had passed the London Matriculation examination in June 1948, in the First Division.

She was an excellent student in every respect, and I am far from being apt to praise inferiority. Her classwork, homework and examination marks were always high; we do not assign positions because of the wide variety of subjects taken, but she was always near the top. I can recall no weak characteristics; she was a good mixer, was invariably hard-working and her conduct was exemplary. She had remarkable powers of concentration, was determined to use her time to the best advantage, and showed a thoughtfulness beyond her years. her character was stable; she gave no evidence of being temperamental, not did she allow her seriousness of purpose to become an obsession. She did much independent reading and during the tutorial classes was never at a loss about what to study.

I have always had a high opinion of her and her work. She has the right temperament and ability to train for the teaching profession.

And on 1st September 1954, Cecil Farthing wrote:

Miss Jana Graf has worked for me during the last five years as a shorthand-typist and secretary.

She is a quick and painstaking worker, and has always been willing to take on jobs other than those which are strictly hers, in order to relieve pressure in the office. She is entirely reliable and honest, diligent and careful. She is a first-rate shorthand-typist.

Our work here is concerned with the official recording of historic buildings in England and Wales, and is largely of an academic nature. I consider Miss Graf would be a most suitable type of student for you to have at San José State College.

Miss Graf has a modest but cheerful and attractive personality, and is certainly above the average in intellectual ability. In initiative she is a good average.

I know nothing of her emotional side; certainly it has never been in evidence in the wear and tear of office life, as she consistently conducts herself with grace and charm.

I shall be sorry to lose her. She is leaving at her own request in order to widen her experience while she is still young.

Both references were received at the Admissions Office, San José State College. They're great references, and might well have secured her the place, but 1954 was also the year when one day Jana happened to be on a ramble in the countryside near Westerham. The direction of her life was about to change yet again.

26

RAMBLING ON LEITH HILL

In 1949, one of Jana's work colleagues had recommended she take a look at the range of evening classes on offer at Morley College. This historic college had been the brainchild of social reformer Emma Cons who had wanted to improve the lot of the residents who lived around Waterloo station towards the end of nineteenth century. She had started weekly 'penny lectures' initially at the Old Vic. Within a few years, Morley College itself had been set up thanks to the financial support of Samuel Morley MP. The college moved to Westminster Bridge Road in 1920, and though much of the building was destroyed in bombing raids during the war, it was soon rebuilt and has continued to expand ever since.

Jana followed her colleague's advice and started attending evening classes. She was soon hooked, and tried out a variety of subjects over the years. An obvious choice for someone like her was music appreciation. Morley had always had a high reputation for all things musical, and Jana enjoyed lectures from such luminaries as Matyas Seiber, Anthony Milner, John Gardner and others. She also followed courses in history, literature and drama, and has continued studying literature to this day, only now she is more likely to attend local classes run by the WEA or U3A. Other classes included Scottish dancing and one about famous figures and their contributions to history.

I used to enjoy going to various events and open days at Morley College as a child, not least because I was entirely captivated by the series of murals on the refectory walls depicting scenes from Chaucer's Canterbury Tales. The originals were painted by Edward Bawden along with Eric Ravilious and Charles Mahoney in 1928. Bawden was paid the princely sum of £1 a day for his work. Unfortunately, the original artworks were destroyed by a bomb raid in 1941. Bawden was invited back to re-create them in 1958, and these are the paintings I've seen and which have inspired me for years. When Jana started attending classes at Morley, the new murals wouldn't yet have been painted, but she was a regular at Morley for a very long time, so must have been there while Bawden was painting version two, though she wasn't aware of this at the time.

As well as the evening classes, Morley also ran Summer schools. Jana attended two of these. One was on *Shakespeare's England*, held at Stratford-upon-Avon, and another explored the seventeenth century and was held just outside Cambridge at Madingley Hall. Jana shared a luxurious on this occasion with another female student. The two of them were about to retire one night when they were informed by the principal that they were sleeping in the very room where Prince Albert had caught his death of cold. He then wished them good night and sent them off to bed. Of course this tale, while not entirely apocryphal, does have holes. Yes, Prince Albert certainly visited Cambridge three weeks before his death in order to sort out the rumours regarding his son, and quite likely did sleep in the very room Jana and her friend were occupying, but he'd been ill for two years, and it was this long term illness that eventually killed him; not the typhoid fever that had been diagnosed at the time, and certainly not a common cold.

While still a student at Regent Street Polytechnic, Jana had spent one summer at a students' farm camp in Norfolk. Life there was very down-to-earth, with the students sleeping in bunks in barns. When the weather was fine, they picked fruit, mainly blackcurrants; while in wet weather they worked in a canning factory. The pay covered bed and board but not much else. As a 'holiday' it probably left a lot to be desired, but once Jana was earning she could leave such working holidays behind and start saving for the real thing. As a keen walker, it made sense to go on holidays with the Ramblers Association, which was well-established by now, having been officially created in 1935. It was on one of these holidays, in Scotland, that she first met Nora Cunningham, a leading light of Morley College Rambling Club. I knew this redoubtable lady in later years as an elderly but tremendously fit and athletic woman with iron grey hair and a winning smile. She told Jana about the Morley College Rambling Club and encouraged her to join, so in one of those odd twists of fate, Nora Cunningham was partially responsible for my own existence. Jana eventually took to walking with the Morley ramblers most Sundays, and also went on further holidays with the Ramblers Association to Austria and Switzerland.

It was with the Morley Ramblers that she met first met my father, Geoff. He had been active in the club since the late 1948, having been introduced to Morley by his older brother Rob. His lifelong friend, Hans Wolff, joined at about the same time. When he was interviewed for a Morley College anniversary publication some years later, Hans spoke of Geoff as a good map reader and dispenser of invaluable information:

Easter weekend 1949 was very mild and sunny, and staying the nights in youth hostels we walked 65 miles in the Cotswolds in three and a half days, in boots which seemed much harder in those days than those of today. To help me deal with the resultant blisters Geoff introduced me to Boots the Chemist's "Foot Comfort" at 6d a tin.

Geoff was a frequent leader of walks, was an active committee member, occasionally organised YHA trips and also the annual dinner and dance – and most memorably for all concerned, the annual photographic competition in which he often won prizes himself, even when someone else took over the organisation. This competition started in 1954 and is still going strong today – and I'm still using one of the cameras with which he took some of his winning photos.

He had been a lifelong rambling enthusiast, having tramped round the local countryside since his early childhood. A love for mountain walking had been kindled when he went for a holiday to Ireland with some friends and saw his first 'real' mountains. He had scrambled up, completely ill-equipped, slipping all the way in shoes with shiny leather soles – but regardless of the difficulties, he was hooked. Later mountain climbing holidays took him to the Dolomites in Italy, but his great love was always for the mountains of Snowdonia and the Lake District fells. If you want to know how he felt about these hills, then read AW Wainwright. In some ways they were kindred spirits, though they never knowingly met. Geoff amassed a huge collection of Wainwright's fell walking guides over the years, like so many walkers of his generation and beyond.

When he and Jana first encountered each other on a Sunday ramble with the Morley group, Geoff was actually dating someone else, but he and Jana soon clicked thanks to their mutual delight in country walking and enthusiasm for all things musical, along with a broadly leftwing political stance. Back in Notting Hill, Maňá gave the relationship her seal of approved. Her comment when she saw Jana covered in mud after a day's ramble was, 'If he can like you when you look like that, he's okay'.

In those days, rumour has it my father was not averse to a drop or two of alcohol. Jana accompanied him one particular evening to a farewell party given by his friend Hans Wolff, who was about to emigrate to Australia. Geoff had been happily mixing his drinks all evening, at the end of which Jana accompanied him as he rolled across the pavement and somehow made it to the railway station. Here she had to leave him – he was going to Croydon, as he was living in Addiscombe, and she was headed in the opposite direction, back to Notting Hill. How he ever got home she doesn't know, and neither did he. He must have gradually grown out of this trait, as in later years he might have enjoyed the odd pint or a shandy when out on a walk, but apart from that his drinking was restricted to the occasional small glass of sherry or ginger wine.

As well as rambling together, Geoff and Jana would often go to promenade concerts, cinema and theatre. Geoff also kept Jana company when she babysat young Charles, and of course they met most Sundays on rambles. He soon introduced Jana to his immediate family: father Henry, stepmother Alice, brothers Rob and Gerry and their wives and children. When Henry died, Jana met more of the relatives at his funeral. I don't know who was at the event, but know from looking at family trees that there could well have been a wealth of cousins and other relations.

For Christmas 1954, Geoff's older brother Rob invited them both to join him and his wife Irene and daughters Ruth and Alison for Christmas dinner. This was Jana's first experience of a full traditional English Christmas dinner. Irene was a very good cook, so Jana was amused when the only part of the main course my cousin Alison would eat was a sausage and baked beans.

Geoff proposed to Jana on a ramble, appropriately enough given the way they'd met, near a pub just outside Westerham in 1954 – and this is where we come back to that photo of Geoff and Jana that appeared on the front page of *The Times*, and which I mentioned near the beginning of this biography. The photo was taken in early 1955. The photographer had apparently been sent to take pictures of some racehorses, but they hadn't materialised so he photographed the most scenic thing he could find – which happened to be the Morley Ramblers tramping down Leith Hill with the famous tower in the background. Jana and Geoff were striding out at the front, so are clearly recognisable in the photo. Jana's boss, who took *The Times*, said that as far as he knew it was the first time a commoner had announced her engagement with a photo in *The Times*.

At around this time they decided to go for a long weekend in Dorset – Jana thinks this was probably Swanage. They arranged to meet at Croydon station, Geoff coming by motorcycle on which they would continue the journey. Jana arrived on her train and waited and waited. She couldn't ring him to see what had happened as she knew Geoff didn't have a phone. She was on the point of returning home when he turned up, having overslept. Their engagement could so easily have ended there. If he'd been a minute later, she would have been tempted to call it a day, though she soon learnt that he tended to leave everything to the last moment.

The wedding took place shortly after the photo appeared, on 26th March 1955 – deliberately timed to be just before the start of the new financial year in order to save on income tax, as neither Geoff – who was working as an office clerk – nor Jana had high incomes. The ceremony took place at Kensington Register Office where the witnesses were Otto and Geoff's brother Rob. They couldn't afford a professional photographer, so one of Geoff's old army pals, Derrick Petts, took the pictures. The wedding cake was baked and beautifully decorated by Geoff's stepmother, Alice.

The reception was held at the glamorous Milestone Hotel overlooking Kensington Gardens. Otto was on tour at the time with the Carl Rosa Opera Company in the north of England and had to come down on an overnight train so had had very little sleep – or as he put it, he must have slept as he woke up many times. He paid for the reception, refusing to let Jana and Geoff contribute. Jana's wedding dress was a couture dress in French navy made by Mrs Brušaková, the former official dressmaker to the wife of Czechoslovak President Beneš. The dress was slim waisted with a wide skirt that hung beautifully thanks to the tiny lead weights sewn into the lining in strategic positions. Jana wore it for 'best' for a while, but when she couldn't fit comfortably into it any more, she re-made it as a skirt, which I wore myself for several years until even my waist couldn't squeeze into it.

The wedding guests included Geoff's immediate family – his father Henry, step-mother Alice, and brothers Rob and Gerry – as well as a number of his army friends. On Jana's side, the guests included Mr and Mrs Somogyi, who were neighbours and friends. Mr Somogyi provided the wedding car as none of the family owned one and Geoff's motorcycle would have been entirely inappropriate. Jana also invited three of her work colleagues along with close pals Erna and Míla Stein. Erna used to take Jana to left-wing political meetings and of course Míla was the mushroom hunter. Regrettably, they didn't feel they could invite their friends from the Morley Rambling Club as they couldn't ask some and not others, and numbers for the wedding and reception were strictly limited. Leo Kersley and his wife couldn't come as they were abroad, but they sent a telegram, as did Hans Wolff, who was by now on a ship bound for Australia.

Geoff and Jana spent their honeymoon in Devon at Bishopsteignton – a place that has since become horribly over-developed, but back then it was an idyllic seaside village. The hotel was the beautiful Regency-style Tapley Manor, which has since been demolished to make way for new housing.

When they returned to London, they moved into rented accommodation in Rose Hill Road, Wandsworth, where they had a bedroom, a living room and a kitchen, plus shared use of a bathroom. The rules limited them to one bath each a week, which sounds draconian but which was not unusual for those times. The accommodation may have been basic, but at least they had beautiful linen, thanks to Elizabeth, Karel Löwner's wife over in the States. Normally the bride's mother would have provided linen for the newlyweds, but as Jana had no mother now, Elizabeth had sent Maňá the money and asked her to buy everything that would be needed. Jana had accompanied Maňá on a shopping trip to choose it all at Whiteleys, the department store in Bayswater which was famous for its linen department.

Geoff was never a gifted linguist, and unfortunately I think I've inherited his skills in this area. In all the years with Jana, he only learnt to say 'máslo prosím' (pass the butter please). He was very proud of this achievement. My knowledge of Czech is no better. My brother and I could have been brought up bi-lingual, but we weren't as Mother decided Czech wasn't a useful language for us to know. Maybe not, but it might have helped with other language acquisition later on. We'll never know. My father also knew how to say *Máš krásné černé oči* (you have beautiful dark eyes). Maňá had taught him to say this to their neighbour in Notting Hill, Rita Somogyi. As he never learnt the Czech word for 'blue' he could never adapt this phrase to use for my mother.

It would have been impossible to raise a family in the two rooms in Wandsworth, so after a while it was time to think about house-hunting. Thanks to Geoff's steady work as an insurance clerk, they were able to take out a mortgage and buy an affordable semi-detached house in Coney Hall, a suburban development right on the edge of London's green belt and not far from Geoff's childhood home in Addiscombe, Croydon. The long garden backed onto woodland, and the walk from the top of the street through the woods and across the fields was one that Geoff's father had taken him on many times as a child. Modern developments have been trying to encroach on the area since the seventies, but it's still possible to do exactly the same walk. I usually manage to do it myself when I go back to visit my mother, who still lives there. Nothing essentially has changed, though the great storm of 1987 that blew down the famous oaks in nearby Sevenoaks has made the woods look far younger than they did when I was a child.

Money was tight, so the motorcycle remained the only mode of transport for a while, though a sidecar was added when my brother and I came along. We even managed to go on holiday like this, apparently – kids and luggage in the sidecar, and parents on the bike. This was obviously impractical, and a four year old Anglia was eventually purchased.

The garden at the house in Coney Hall was very long and narrow and needed a new fence. This was financed in an unexpected way. Through a London based solicitor who specialised in international law, Jana was able to be part of a class action against Germany for loss of freedom and having to wear the yellow star. The claim was for 36 months at 150DM per month a total of 5400DM. This was worth £459 when the claim was made in July 1960. The solicitor's fee was £45 18s 9d, so Jana received a total of £407 1s 9d, which more than paid for the new fence.

Much later, she also received compensation from the *Generali Fund in Memory of Generali Insured in East and Central Europe who perished in the Holocaust*. Gustav had taken out two life policies with Generali Insurance Co, and the three beneficiaries were Paul, Jana and Charles. They each received $3679 in June 2003. This was an ex-gratia payment – a goodwill gesture by the company. According to their records, the policies had matured in 1939 and 1940, but nothing had been received. This compensation was organised by the *International Commission on Holocaust Era Insurance Claims*, based in Jerusalem.

The house in Birch Tree Avenue, Coney Hall is where I grew up thinking everyone had long gardens full of fruit trees, just as my mother must have thought in her own childhood that everyone had access to such places, and always would. I always imagined everyone went on a walk on a Sunday afternoon; everyone knew which mushrooms you could pick and eat; everyone's mother knew dozens of recipes for bottling fruit and making jam.

There the similarities end. Coney Hall is no Bratislava. There are no grand buildings, no opera houses, no theatres; no coffee shops full of men smoking cigars and swapping stamps; but there are gardens; there are sparrows chirping outside the window – though not so many these days – there are woods and meadows, and you can even fly a kite should you feel so inclined. You can go on walks and pick bilberries and blackberries; you can climb apple trees and run up and down the lawn and play with the kids next door to your heart's content. London isn't too far away, so theatres and galleries are within easy reach.

I grew up in a house full of music. My brother and I and our dad all played the piano, and I took up the violin, eventually becoming a professional musician. My mother might not have had the skills to sing Schubert to us instead of nursery rhymes, but at least Dad could play Haydn and Brahms. My brother and I collected stamps; and I danced. We occasionally went out in small boats, but we never came up against a gate that wouldn't open. We were never stuck in a frightening place, not knowing if we would escape. We were never in any doubt that we would survive.

And as I write that last sentence, by pure chance an absolutely spine-tingling performance of the archetypal Czech symphony, Dvořak's seventh, is playing on the radio, conducted, appropriately enough, by little Martin's father – Rafael Kubelik.

APPENDIX I

Maňá's letter to Karel regarding Paul. Written in Czech, translated into English by Jana.

Dearest Karel,

First of all I apologise for answering only now after such a long pause. I explained it more or less to dear Elizabeth – the reason had nothing to do with poor health, on the contrary I have been feeling very well all the time, but I am so busy that bye the evenings when I should have time, I feel so tired that in spite of best intentions I can't concentrate on letter-writing. I hope you are not angry with me, but believe me that sometimes things get on top of me.

Thank you wholeheartedly for the cheque – it's very kind of you and believe me I find your kindness very touching. Of course it came extremely useful as lately I've had lots of expenses and of course I don't have an income at present. I used to have a decent salary but now I will happily economise as I am so happy to have the little creature. We didn't even send you a telegram to announce the happy event as I couldn't send it from the hospital and Ota, as usual, was away. Our biggest problem now is our flat. It is hopeless living in two small rooms and for some months I have spent most of my time looking for a larger flat. Unfortunately, so far without luck, and so all of us are crowded together. But now Ota will be in London for some time and so he will take the job on. We thought that Paul will shortly leave to join you but there appears to be another hitch, First of all there were difficulties to find a place on a ship; with great difficulty I found someone who (of course with financial inducement) promised that he could sail in mid-October, and when we showed this in black and white at the American Consulate we were told that although Paul's documents are O.K., the Czechoslovak quota, under which he comes, is full and so he would not be able to travel for another six or eight months. That was quite a blow. It means that he would waste a year. He can't enter a school here as it is too late to enrol – no college would now take him not even for some short course. Everything lasts at least a year and is very expensive and money would be wasted as he would not finish the year. So it has been decided that he will go to a farm and so kill two birds with one stone – he will need to speak English in which he is not proficient (can't be compared with Hana), also he will be in fresh air which he doesn't get in London. For his height he is very thin so perhaps physical activity will do him good. I wondered if he might be able to get to USA earlier on a student's visa. Do you think you could chase up Paul's case from your end? Just a letter appealing to people's humanity is useless. I have sent plenty to the consul and never got a reply. Naturally it does not increase Paul's self-confidence and what makes it worse that Hana attends school and is preparing for matriculation (London University) which she will take in two years. I had many influential friends who could have helped with the American Consulate. Unfortunately they have all gone back to Czechoslovakia and so I am quite helpless. The place on the boat cannot now be used and so it will all have to start again. There are always difficulties with booking a berth.

So that is the whole situation. How much easier life would be if we all lived closer to each other. Although we are quite a large family, I often feel very alone and so I think more and more about you. We have still not decided whether to stay here or return to our homeland. There are many pros and contras. I think it will have to be decided during the year. It is possible that Ota will go to America to sing in Britten's new Opera "Rape of Lucretia". It is still long way away and not certain. So far he hasn't yet been to Czechoslovakia – will go there some time in the New Year.

So, for today I say good-bye. Hoping to hear from you soon and once again heartfelt thanks.

Kisses from your
Maňá.

APPENDIX II

Memoir written by Marian Tracy (daughter of Elizabeth and Karel Loewner), based on her mother's account of emigration to the United States.

Tracing an Old Path.

'The city of Louisville is a beautiful, cultured big city with attractive houses and wide streets, not at all wild-west like.' This was my mother's description of our new Kentucky house. Together with my father and me, a child of three, she had just arrived from Prague, Czechoslovakia, in November of 1939.

Though in time she altered her view of Louisville, it was initially a jolt to discover that not every American town could be used as a set for a Western movie. My parents had been advised before coming to this country that they should learn horseback riding. However, they discovered that, far more useful than equestrian skills, was the knowledge of how to drive a car.

At the time they possessed neither skill. Except for the wealthy, feet were definitely the means of transportation in the pre-war European city. They were supplemented by trolleys.

My father, who had been selected to head the Department of Mathematics at the University of Prague, had been hired by the University of Louisville. His heavy teaching assignment, consisting entirely of elementary courses, would be frowned upon by most beginning

212

instructors today. However, college positions, like any others, were scarce and he felt fortunate to get one.

His salary was paid by a wealthy lawyer of the area whose hobby was collecting original manuscripts of mathematical works. An agreement was made by which the lawyer would reimburse the university for my father's salary in exchange for receiving an original manuscript of a work of Albert Einstein.

Getting out of Europe had not been easy. It had taken months of standing in lines to get application forms approved by the Gestapo. One mistake could mean that all papers would be invalidated and the whole procedure would have to be repeated. My father had been beaten because he had lost a small piece of paper with a number used to direct traffic in a building.

We were the only members of our immediate family to leave. Among those we were hoping to bring to this country were my mother's parents, two brothers and two sisters of my father, one brother-in-law and later on, another sister and her family.

Between the time of our arrival and the time of U.S. entry into World War II numerous family letters passed back and forth across the Atlantic. They were stamped by both American and German censors and the sign of the swastika was to be found on every envelope. Very small handwriting or typing on both sides of thin paper make these German letters difficult to read. they travelled slowly. Sometimes it took weeks for an air mail letter to get through. Because so many were lost in transit, the writers often kept copies so that they could repeat what had been said. These letters have sharpened the edges of my vague memories and brought to life the trying days of forty years ago.

'I wouldn't have thought seasickness is something so unpleasant,' wrote my mother, describing our voyage on the Dutch ship, Staatendam. It had had a rough passage and was accompanied by British ships through the English Channel to steer it clear of mines. 'I was so sick for six days that I couldn't eat and sometimes couldn't even stay upright.

The last day on board we had to stand in line for eight hours in order to have our papers checked.'

We were not certain who if anyone would meet us at the docks and we had no money. It was therefore a pleasant surprise to be greeted by Professor Von Neuman, a mathematician from Princeton University who had been informed of our coming. With change in our pockets we were whisked off to Princeton after only a glimpse of New York.

In Princeton we visited many people, some of whom had names known to my parents. Three days later we were put on a train bound for Louisville.

A short time after our arrival my mother observed that everything she had seen so far in the United States reminded her of pre-war Germany, from where she originally came. There seemed to be a greater similarity between two countries at peace than between the same country at peace and at war. (She had seen her parents in Germany that year.) All differences were nebulous at first. America was to be her home. Perhaps for this reason she was trying to adjust to this idea by noting similarities rather than differences.

However, she quickly changed her emphasis. About a month later she wrote, 'Almost everything is different even from a superficial point of view. Houses are built differently. They are lower and wider. Lights are more colourful and burn more brightly. An unending stream of cars fills the streets. The private houses have little gardens but no fences separate them from each other or from the streets.

'Downtown consists only of stores, especially auto shops and little department stores called five and tens, where one can get anything. Of course they don't have first class merchandise but for people with little money, which means us, quite good. Book stores and music stores are hardly to be found but on every corner is a drugstore, which is like an all around servant. You can get not only drugs but ice cream and other things to eat, newspapers, tobacco and sweets.

'Furniture is different from what we imagined it to be. Everything is Baroque imitation. Our plain simple furniture is almost impossible to find.

'Mealtimes are hard to get used to. Americans generally eat a light cold lunch about noon and don't really eat until six in the evening. We get headaches from running around so long without having anything decent to eat. Maybe in the heat of the summer it is better that way. Should anyone come to the U.S. A. he has to bring me a wooden spoon and whisk. Such things don't exist here.' This request is repeated in a number of letters. Sometimes when there are many adjustments to make it is easy to focus on relatively minor things.

'The people are very different from the people at home. they have never seen a war or at least not for a long time and they know no worries. They are therefore of a cheerfulness that seems rather alien to us right now, so much so that we feel like misplaced persons. One absolutely does not want to hear anything about troubles. The opinion seems to be that one should be glad to be here and forget one's troubles as quickly as possible. It is absolutely necessary to respond to the question, "How are you?" with, "Very fine," or all conversation ceases. The people are gracious but it doesn't really come from the heart.'

My parents continued to have mixed feeling about the friendliness and helpfulness of the Louisvillians. They were astounded and moved by their reception upon their arrival. An assistant of the president of the university, a young German professor who acted as an interpreter, a news reporter and a photographer greeted us at the train station as the result of a telegram someone had sent, notifying them of our coming. Later the president brought roses to our apartment. the letter in which this was related had to be interrupted because of this surprise visit.

On the other hand she expected much more help than we got in bringing over our family. She discussed these problems with everyone with whom she came into contact, emphasising our need for affidavits. According to her no one

215

offered any help, only 'nice words'. Particularly disappointing was the lack of response from Jewish organisations. (The last I remember hearing from my parents. It was not dealt with in the letters.) Had the people been less friendly she would have expected less. An engineer at the university did make out an affidavit for one of my father's brothers.

Three weeks after coming to Kentucky my father was to start teaching. He knew almost no English. However, through a concentrated effort he was able to do it and four months later, according to my mother, he hardly had to prepare. It was personal conversation that was difficult. 'We have made progress,' my mother relates, 'especially in mastering the Kentucky dialect'.

'Social life at the university is very active,' she writes. 'One lives in one's house and entertains there. Since there aren't any real coffee houses people depend on the house to house traffic. The only difficulties are with small children. Every month there is a dinner held for people belonging to the Speed Scientific School (Engineering School) where the men meet at one restaurant and the women at another but after that they get together at a private home. With cars all this isn't too difficult. Then I also belong to a music club (my mother had for some years been a professional singer in Europe) and to the Newcomers Club. It seems like at every moment there's a lunch or dinner given by some group or organization, ie Speed School, Liberal Arts School, student organisations, with speeches, usually about education. all this is a good opportunity to learn English.

'Private invitations also abound. Last Sunday we were visited by five families with children at our small apartment and next Sunday we're invited again so we certainly are not alone. Maybe all this active social life is a result of Louisville's being a small town where cohesion is greater.'

Louisville was at the time a city of about 300,000, hardly a small town. Perhaps she vaguely thought that any

216

town in which the people are friendly cannot be called a big city. Some grounds for this conclusion might be found by examining her impressions of New York City, which we visited for the first time in the summer of 1940. She was impressed by the skyscrapers, churches, Hudson river and harbour but much less enamoured of the people she met on the streets. 'The big city,' my mother wrote, 'destroys honesty, decency and simple humanity.' She preferred the citizens of Louisville with their friendliness and helpfulness.

During that summer we spent part of the time in Hanover, New Hampshire. My father accepted an invitation to Dartmouth College so that we could escape the Louisville summer heat and he would have the opportunity to be near the good mathematical library there. Upon our return my mother wrote, 'For ten days we are back in Louisville, which is not exactly an ugly city and where the people are much more pleasant than in the East but which has a climate which is absolutely dreadful. We again suffer from the heat, which makes us too tired to do any real work. The climate of the U.S. A. you can hardy imagine. Everywhere people try to make drafts to get a little air. Houses stand separately in order to create drafts. Only the Blacks, who do all the heavy work, don't seem to suffer. We Europeans, of course, suffer more under the heat more than the Americans but even they moan and groan and everyone talks about it. Europe has to credit its intellectual accomplishments largely to its good climate.'

Something my parents sorely missed were the long walks through the woods of Germany and Czechoslovakia. 'Since everyone has a car there are only highways and those aren't too pleasant to walk along. We dream of walking long hours through woods,' says my mother. I recall some of our attempts to walk along highways during which we were repeatedly offered a ride. Usually we gave up trying to walk and hitchhiked. Some of our walks took us through Black neighbourhoods, which we dubbed Africa, where we were decidedly looked upon as curiosities.

Early in 1941 we were really in the thick of Louisville University social activities. My mother writes, 'The usual meeting of the Speed Scientific School was held this time at our apartment and I set myself up as speaker, giving a lecture to the ladies about Prague. A lot of preparations for such an event are unnecessary. Usually there is a cold drink consisting of fruit juice with ice water (every Frigidaire creates that and every house has a Frigidaire) and some dessert. With the help of my friend I already had all the glasses filled except for the icewater and placed on trays. I also had rounded up all the chairs in the apartment house and with the aid of an opaque projector, loaned from a physics professor, and a book about Prague, which is one of the few belletristic books we took with us as a remembrance, was able to show the Americans the beautiful old buildings of our Czech homeland. About old things they are always enthusiastic.'

Most of that year, however, my parents were preoccupied with attempts to bring over the family. To her parents my mother wrote, 'Your letters are always moving and a great joy to us. Hopefully you will stay healthy and our great desire to see you again will reach fulfilment. When? Where? That nobody knows today. For my part I hope it is not in Louisville as the climate and lack of money oppress us a great deal. However, you know that I don't give up hope easily and often dream that you are sitting around the table with us.' Most letters contain similar words and sentiments.

The sisters and brothers of my father were considering that it would probably be necessary to leave Europe and some were learning other skills and professions from those they were practising. One brother who was in banking was taking a course in architecture and a sister who was a secretary was learning cosmetology in preparation for coming to this country. We had communicated to them, the advisability of doing this as we were told it that it would be easer to get employment in these fields at the time.

Nevertheless, one doesn't detect any sense of urgency on their part. Whether or not they retained their jobs seemed more important to them. Several of them were taking vacations in the vicinity of Prague.

My parents' communication of their general depression might have been a bit discouraging. 'Altogether our life here isn't as ideal as you imagine,' my mother wrote. 'There are a lot of disappointments, useless work, humiliations and vexations. Our life was pleasanter in former times.

'Immigrants here live in rather sorry circumstances, are very much exploited and badly paid. Americans like to give charity but not jobs. In addition, immigrants must be modest and by all means not know more than the Americans. That they can't stand in the least. According to our friends from Prague (living in Boston) modesty does not work in this country. Here one must advertise oneself, run a big house, talk about oneself.' Though there appears to be a direct contradiction in these statements there seems to be some truth in both. Many people feel that they must walk a tightrope to 'get ahead' without causing resentment and envy. For immigrants like my parents the rope must have been especially thin.

'In effect we don't have half as much income as we thought we would have. More than any figures could show is the fact that Karl's salary is $400 below the level at which taxes begin to b paid. In addition, we don't live as immigrants usually do. Instead we have many more social obligations than in Prague. Other immigrants have it a lot worse but they can live simpler lives.'

In spite of his dissatisfaction with his position my father was worried that he would not be allowed to continue teaching. My parents apparently seemed to think that participation in social life was imperative to my father's retaining his job.

'All in all,' my mother continued, 'America is really not at all suitable for Karl and certainly not Louisville. Not one professor here works scientifically (does research). Mainly they have to teach and grade papers, giving grades even for homework. It's worst than high school in Europe.'

219

Because of his heavy teaching schedule and having to grade papers several hours a day my father did not have time to do research, which he had done for years. (In Europe he had made some significant contributions to mathematics.) This was, other than anxiety over the family, the primary cause of his depression.

He was, however, a devoted teacher. At one point some of his students requested that he hold a seminar for a semester so that they could learn more about mathematics than they were getting in the regular courses. The university gave permission for this only under the condition that it be held at seven o'clock in the morning and that it be unpaid My father agreed. When it was decided that because of the success of the seminar its conductor should be paid it was taken over by someone else. This professor did not even consult with my father.

'There are many disappointments and heartaches,' my mother wrote concerning our efforts to affect the immigration of our relatives. 'Unfortunately we don't as yet have an affidavit for Viktor because the generosity of the Americans seems to have stopped It was already confirmed and then withdrawn. Everything is much more complicated now. One needs to fill out more papers and forms and run around more. But if one can thereby accomplish something one is glad to do it. On the positive side I learned from the Social Help that the Czech quota was enlarged and opened. Is this known in Prague?'

One sister wrote back, 'We are not surprised that affidavit generosity has declined. Everything exhausts itself eventually. About an opening in the Czech quota we know nothing. I don't think we can undertake anything now. All our thoughts about emigrating end with a question mark. Should we think about it? What should be done? Should we do something? One lets come what may. Don't worry about us. Hopefully everything will come out all right.'

Another letter from Europe contains the following lines. 'The trip to the U.S.A. is as you say easier. It no longer depends on the quota number. The main thing is to have in one's possession tickets for a certain ship on a certain day. It is certain that until June all ships leaving Lisbon are fully booked. In addition one's affidavit has to be valid. It means, practically speaking, that it would still take a very long time after all formalities are taken care of to actually be on the way to the U.S.A. Also, the affidavits, though good until March, 1943, might have to have new verifications.'

In April of 1941 my parents wrote, 'One person may now make out numerous affidavits to next of kin.' By the beginning of summer the affidavits had been sent to all the sisters and brothers. However, one brother wrote back, 'Only two of the affidavits can be used as there are age restrictions on those permitted to emigrate. Only a certain number of people within an age group can leave.'

On the whole, however, the situation seemed to be more hopeful. My father had secured a low interest bank loan through the university. We were informed that the money could be sent through the Join Distribution Committee to the Kultusgemeinder in Prague with the stipulation that it be used for the tickets for designated persons. Part of the fare could be paid in Czech crowns, making it possible for them to contribute.

Toward the end of 1941 attempts were made to bring the family across through Mexico or Cuba. These routes had been available throughout 1940 and 1941 but it seems my parents had not been aware of them. Letters were replaced by telegrams. On December 4, 1941, a telegram notified the relatives that Cuban visas had been obtained and that all financial transactions had been made. Three days later all efforts came to a halt with Pearl Harbor.

Failure to bring about a reunion with the family put my parents into a deep depression. When notification came that her parents had been sent to Theresienstadt my mother sobbed uncontrollably. That is the only time that I can recall her crying. Since 1933, immediately after Hitler came to power, she told them that they must leave Germany. After the war we found out that only one brother, who had a Gentile wife, survived the concentration camps.

The kaleidoscope of changing rules and procedures certainly seemed to confuse and discourage those on both sides of the Atlantic who were trying to get Jews out of Europe. The channels would probably have widened and cleared more quickly had the consequences been known. However, today one can still see similar results of impeded relief efforts caused by red tape and bureaucratic confusion.

In discussion of the Nazi holocaust there is always the nagging question of whether more resistance of the part of the Jews in Europe would have resulted in fewer deaths. Much has been said on this issue, and of course one can only speculate on past consequences. However, I vividly recall that my mother told me about the way she had stood up to an S.S. man at a critical point. One day during an inspection of our application forms for emigration she was asked because of a supposed error to drop the papers into the wastebasket. Instead of complying, which would have cost us months of vaulable time, she looked at the man squarely and said simply, 'I cannot do that. I have a child.' A bullet could easily have been the response but the man only opened his mouth in surprise and let her pass. She may have been lucky, but probably because of her courage I am here to write about it.

Marian Tracy

APPENDIX III

RECIPES

Knedliky

There are two types of knedliky: bread and potato.

Bread knedliky
Ingredients
4oz plain flour
4 oz semolina
about ¼ pint milk
4 oz stale bread
one egg yolk (whole egg if making double quantity)
salt

Method
Mix to make a thick batter of all the ingredients apart from the bread. Leave to stand for an hour or more. Cut the bread into 1cm cubes, the day before if too fresh. Form into one large cylindrical dumpling with wet hands. Drop into boiling water and cook for half an hour, turning after a few minutes. It should rise to the top when done. If making double quantity, wait until the water has returned to the boil before dropping in the second one. Use strong cotton to cut into 1cm thick slices, and dribble with melted butter.

Potato knedliky:
Ingredients
1½ lb boiled and peeled potatoes
10oz flour and semolina mixed

two eggs
salt
1tbsp vinegar

Method
Grate the cold potatoes, mix in other ingredients, form into four cylinders, and boil in salted water for about twenty minutes. Slice, dribble with butter, and enjoy.

Knedliky are delicious served with boiled beef and dill sauce.

For the beef, take a sizeable chunk of beef – brisket is ideal. Cook in 1½ to 2 pints of water in a pressure cooker with salt, peppercorns, quartered onions, whole garlic, carrots, celery, parsley and mace.

For the sauce, make a roux, dilute with the beef stock, flavour with a little vinegar and brown sugar. When nearly done, add a generous handful of chopped mint and some sour cream or thick plain yogurt.

Kočiči oči (cat's eyes)

Ingredients
125g plain flour
125g self-raising flour
130g castor sugar
1 egg
vanilla essence
lemon rind
130g butter
jam (redcurrant jelly works well)
icing sugar

Method
Rub the butter into the dry ingredients. Add the egg and vanilla and mix well. Leave in the fridge to harden. Roll out very thinly. Cut into circles, half with a small hole cut out in the centre. Bake on a greased tray in a moderate oven until just starting to colour. Allow to cool, then sandwich together with the jam. Dust with icing sugar.

Apple Buchty

Ingredients
1 egg
1 lb plain flour
2 oz butter, melted, plus extra for brushing
1 oz fresh yeast (or ½ oz dried)
about ⅓ pint warm milk
½ tsp salt
vanilla essence

Apple puree (made with Bramley apples, a little sugar, flavoured with lemon rind)

Method
Activate the fresh yeast by blending with a little sugar and leaving with some of the warm milk until it's frothy, or use the dried as per packet instructions. Mix all the dough ingredients together, beat well, leave to rise. Take tablespoons of the risen dough, pat out, put in some apple puree and wrap round to make a parcel. Put the buchty in a greased tin. Brush with melted butter between them, and don't place too close. Leave to rise. Brush tops with melted butter and bake in a fairly hot oven for ten minutes; then reduce heat and cook for another 30 – 35 minutes. Turn out and separate. Leave to cool.

Vánočka

Ingredients
120g butter
2 eggs
vanilla essence
¼ litre warm milk
50g sultanas
50g chopped almonds or mixed nuts
110g caster sugar
grated lemon rind
25 fresh yeast (or half if using dried)
500g strong plain flour and semolina mixed
50g candied peel
vanilla sugar for sprinkling

Method
Beat together the butter and the sugar. Add one whole egg and one yolk, the lemon rind and vanilla, and beat well. Add the flour, and the yeast sponged in some of the milk (or according to the packet instructions if using dried), and the rest of the milk a bit at a time – this should be a fairly stiff dough. Knead thoroughly. Knead in the fruit, peel and nuts. Leave to rise in a warm place until more or less doubled in size.

Divide into eight equal pieces. Form seven pieces into long sausages. Plait four of the sausages together. Lay on a foil lined tray. Brush with egg white. Plait the three remaining sausages and lay on top of the first plait. Brush with egg white. Divide the eighth piece of dough in half and form into two thin sausages. Twist together and lay on top. Secure with cocktail sticks if it looks like it might topple. Brush all over with egg white. Bake for up to twenty minutes in a fairly hot oven, then cover lightly with baking parchment to stop it singeing, reduce the heat, and continue baking for another forty minutes or so. Remove from oven and sprinkle with baking sugar.

Acknowledgments

Many thanks to Jana Tanner, Paul G Loewner, Marian Tracy and Gerda Kolar for their invaluable first hand accounts; Daniel Abelman for translations and research; and Kay Green and the team at Earlyworks Press for all their advice, encouragement and help in writing this book.

wormwood, earth and honey

selected poems by Catherine Edmunds

Accessible but never trivial; warm, earthy intelligent
and – just when you begin to snuggle into the intimacy
of it – spiked with fire and venom.

Paperback ISBN 978-1-90645104-2
Illustrated ebook edition ISBN 978-1-906451-27-1

Small Poisons

a novel by
Catherine Edmunds

A contemporary novel for Midsummer Night's dreamers

Lulled into a sense of false security, the reader might begin to think he/she is in an enchanted garden full of beauty, magic and kindness. As the dream turns into nightmare, we discover otherwise The author has created a world that is rreal, terrifying and yet totally believable.

– Mandy Pannett

Paperback ISBN 978-1-906451-16-5
ebook ISBN 9781-906451-41-7

Serpentine

a novel by
Catherine Edmunds

Painting isn't a job – it's the reason for Victoria's very existence – so how is she to bridge the gap between her art and her private life? José givesw her the intensity she craves, but has no interest in her as an artist. Simon offers a mature and loving relationship, but his gentleness and inability to understand her compulsions drive her to distraction. And the there's John – a man who understands exactly who she is, but unnerves her with his perspicacity and potentially violent nature. Vicgtoria's friend Emma has bruises on her face and Victoria thinks she knows who put them there.

Paperback ISBN 978-1-906451-63-9
ebook ISBN 978-1-906451-62-2

Bacchus Wynd

a novel by
Catherine Edmunds

Emma is fascinated by an Impressionist seascape in a local gallery. Grains of sand are caught forever in the paint – trapped, just as she is in a claustrophobic relationship with John. Each week the two of them meet ther friends in the café on the corner of Bacchus Wynd; each week Emma is convinced that Toby is her only means of escape – but Evan is watching, and he knows Toby's secret.

Meanwhile, John's life is falling apart. Renée senses the impending crisis, but is well aware of how hard he is to help. And what of her own feelings, torn between the compulsion to resurrect an old affair, and a growing desire for Toby?

As each struggles with increasingly fraught emotions, Toby fills his head with facts, believing one day he'll know enough of them not to be frightened of anything – but his strategy isn't working.

The next two weeks will change everything.

Paperback ISBN 978-1-906451-93-6
ebook ISBN 978-1-906451-94-3